Sheffield Workhouse

MARGARET DRINKALL

The History Press

First published 2011

The History Press
The Mill, Brimscombe Port
Stroud, Gloucestershire, GL5 2QG
www.thehistorypress.co.uk

British Library Cataloguing in Publication Data.
A catalogue record for this book is available from the British Library.

ISBN 978 0 7524 5963 9

Typesetting and origination by The History Press
Printed in Great Britain

Sheffield Workhouse

Contents

Introduction

Following the publication of the *Rotherham Workhouse* in 2009, I became intrigued by the idea of researching Sheffield's workhouse. The Rotherham Guardians' Minutes state quite clearly that the only workhouse which they had difficulties working with was the one at Sheffield. In November 1851, it was noted in the Minutes that 'this Board laments that their endeavours to come to a good understanding with the Sheffield Board of Guardians have been in vain'. I can see why they came to that conclusion: the Guardians were not only a contentious and argumentative group of men as far as internal disputes went, but also, on several occasions, warred with officials from other workhouses. For example, the local newspaper reported on 5 November 1859 that 'a very long, noisy, personal and very absurd altercation took place regarding an order which had been made for 5 dozen boys' caps when there were only 4 dozen boys in the house'. One of the Guardians stated, at a Board meeting, that 'the proceedings of the Board of Guardians as reported in the newspapers have been disgraceful to Sheffield'. As the Guardians were elected on a yearly basis for most of the time of this research, why these disputes should keep arising on each successive Board is a mystery to this author. It seems that Sheffield Guardians were not exceptional in this type of behaviour, however, as it was reported in April 1900 that the Gainsborough Guardians came to blows during one of their meetings.

Fierce resistance had been experienced in Sheffield and other areas of Yorkshire to the introduction of the Poor Law Amendment Act – which demanded that the workhouse system be centralised and standardised – and to the election of the Guardians themselves. Commentators at the time stated that if they succumbed to this Act, 'they would be slaves for ever'. Resistance was also seen to the erection of the various workhouses in Sheffield on many occasions and several large meetings were held by the ratepayers of the town against the Poor Law authorities. None was more loud in their criticisms of the Poor Law Commission (which later became the Poor Law Board and finally the Local Government Board) than the Sheffield Guardians themselves. They saw the Poor Law authorities as being intent on forcing the Act on Sheffield. Rotherham elected their Guardians quietly, but the men of Sheffield were more hardy souls and held out until it was emphasized, as a point of law, that they had no option but to obey the edicts of the Act.

No images of this type survive for Sheffield, but this photograph shows the type of people who were admitted to workhouses across the country every day.

But my interest has always been in the inmates themselves and in the lives they led inside and outside of the workhouse. As a rule, inmates were only named in the records as a result of bad behaviour or because enquiries were being made into the Guardians' practices. These mostly unnamed residents of Sheffield's workhouses were roundly condemned by both the ratepayers and the Guardians alike. They regarded them, almost without exception, as being 'composed of vagabonds who were too idle to work'.

But in Sheffield's Archives I have discovered two letter books which tell us more about the lives of the inmates themselves. Conditions in an industrial town such as Sheffield were dire, and the many periods of industrial distress – or the many epidemics which afflicted the town – reveal lives filled with poverty and squalor. Many people had to make a decision either to go into the workhouse or to starve; children had no choice at all. But what the books reveal more than anything is that the inmates were respectable people brought 'down on their luck'. For example, the Guardians themselves point out the hardship of a family who once ran a public house in York who, through debt, were now in the Kelham Street workhouse. Thankfully, the letter books hold some case histories of the people who came into Sheffield workhouse and what happened to them there. I would suggest that people interested in the lives of paupers take a look at these letter books, which are mostly quite readable. At the end of this book I list the names of some of the paupers mentioned, and some sources for family historians, as well as a full bibliography.

Most of the early records of the Sheffield workhouse were destroyed during the bombing of the town during the Second World War. The only Guardians' Minutes which survive are from 1890. However, by using Parish Council Minutes, trade directories, workhouse material in the archives and the local newspapers, I have managed to research the development of the workhouse in Sheffield. The research was further complicated by the fact that there was more than one workhouse operating in Sheffield at the same time. There were also two farms operating to employ men on out-relief and a school for the children at Pitsmoor. It has been impossible to research all the workhouses and so I have concentrated on the main Sheffield workhouse on Kelham Street (later at Fir Vale). The geography of Sheffield inevitably meant that names of workhouses or areas were interchangeable. For example, the children's schools at Pitsmoor were variously called Brightside and Pitsmoor. The piece of land bought by the Guardians was stated to be at both Handsworth and Darnall, so, for ease, I have used my own judgment where possible. I apologise for any mistakes, which are my own. I have also used the terms 'imbeciles and lunatics' as they were written and with no intention to offend any readers. Sheffield received its Municipal Charter to become a city in 1893, but for ease I have used the term 'town' throughout. I have also limited the research to end in the Victorian period as after that time workhouses were moving towards hospital status and the fear of entering the workhouse's portals was diminishing for many Sheffield people.

I am extremely grateful to Shirley Miller of the Kelham Island Museum for permission to use several previously unpublished illustrations of the Kelham Street workhouse before it was demolished in 1945. The original pictures were taken by Woodhead Components Ltd of Globe Steel Works, who I have been unable to trace: however, if they contact me I will happily rectify the omission in my next book. I would like to sincerely thank the staff at the Sheffield Archives and Library Service for their unfailing help during the research for this book as well as for the superb illustrations from the Archives and the 'Picture Sheffield' series. They were, without exception, kind and knowledgeable, and often made suggestions about where further material about the workhouse could be found. I am also very grateful to the staff at The History Press, without whom this book would never have been written. Last – but definitely not least – to my son Chris, for all his help with the illustrations and for his encouragement and 'ongoing support' (only another four and a half years to go, Chris!). I am most grateful to the readers who buy this book, and I hope that you enjoy reading about the Sheffield workhouse as much as I have enjoyed writing about it.

Margaret Drinkall, 2011

one

The Early Workhouse

From time immemorial, feeding for and caring for the poor were responsibilities undertaken by religious houses. Only after the Reformation did this become a parish responsibility. The people who were charged with the care of the poor of Sheffield were the Town Burgesses or Trustees, and I am indebted to the Records of the Burgery of Sheffield for much of the following information. An early map outlines the properties owned in Sheffield by the Town Trustees against those owned by the Church. A Charter had been granted to the Trustees as early as 1297 from the Duke of Norfolk to ensure that a body of men was elected yearly to overlook their parish tasks. These would include not only caring for the sick and poor but they would also have the responsibility of ensuring roads were passable, rubbish was cleared from the streets and enforcing law and order. Unfortunately, little evidence remains of their dealings with the poor of the town apart from the account entries, where it seems that payments were made to cover a multitude of needs. Some of the payments listed were:

1567: Item payde for goynge about the towne to write the pore people, 5*d*
1569: Item gev to John Horner for the caryeage of a pore man to the constables, 3*d*
1570: Given to Thomas Woods wife for helping to set two of her children to service, 6*s* 8*d*
1573: To Oates wife, wyddcwe being verye syck and almost famished for lacke of foode to her selfe and her children, 15*d*
1585: Item payde for a sheet to wynde a poor boye that Dyed in the towne, 11*d*

The Trustees were able to make these payments through the charity of philanthropic people of the town who left money and property to use for the relief of the poor. In 1570, rents were obtained from the people of the town which went into the parish coffers and were listed thus:

Thomas Phyllyps, 3*d*
George Morton, 1s 2*d*
William Sklatter, 1*d*

Thomas Wille, 1s

Roger Buttwods, 20d

Thomas Dots, 1s 1d

George Kendall, 1s 5d

Hugh Streye, 16d

Elen Yowle, 1s 5d

The Shemelle House, 5s

Thomas Spencer, 2d

Thomas Horner, 5d

These records give a fascinating picture of life in Sheffield in these early years and particularly of the terrible poverty in which many people lived. In researching these documents we find that the town had a pillory and a ducking stool, both used as a form of punishment. The pillory was erected in 1635 and cost 25s. A pillory was similar to the stocks, except that the victim would stand, with their head and hands inserted through holes (rather than just the feet). These were uncomfortable, as the prisoner was in a standing position for sometimes hours on end. The prisoner suffered the same punishment as in the stocks in that rotten vegetables, eggs and soft fruit were thrown at the miscreant. There is no indication of where these stocks were erected, but they were usually placed in the centre of the town to ensure that the prisoner would be humiliated and would not offend again. The ducking stool, which was used exclusively on women, was made the same year as there is listed a payment 'for cuck stool, 2 cheynes and 2 locks amounting to 13s'. This was a seat in which the woman was paraded through the streets, or lowered into a pond, usually after charges were brought against her that she was a nag, a gossip or a witch. We know that this form of barbaric punishment was still happening in 1747, when a sum of 1s was paid for 'getting the cuck stool out of the river'.

Historically, even poor men were forced to develop their skills in archery, as demanded by the Crown, as a defensive army for times of war. In the Burgery accounts it states in 1634 that 'every parish in the land is bound by law to have and to exercise with long bows at holidays and other times convenient'. There was even 'a township bow' which the poor men of the town might use and which regularly needed re-stringing. The archery butts were set up on the Wicker and they were repaired in 1642 at a cost of 3s. The upkeep of the butts and the repair of them were the responsibility of the town Trustees.

Early recipients of relief would have been given whatever they required in their own home. This was called 'outdoor relief', and could take the form of rent, bread or funeral costs. The Poor Law Act of 1601 required that workhouses be built for the 'impotent poor'; in return for this largesse they would have to work, a system to be known as 'indoor relief'. The records show that there was already a workhouse in the town in 1629, when 'part of the site of the present workhouse' was to be used as an open space for the townspeople (towards which the Trustees contributed £100). A letter from Mr Hugh Parker, asking the townspeople to start a subscription to purchase the entire site, was received at a town meeting the following year. Once again the Trustees subscribed £200 towards the scheme. It is probable that the entire site was bought, because a new workhouse was opened by 1632 and the rent was 10s a year. The accounts also show that some thought was given to

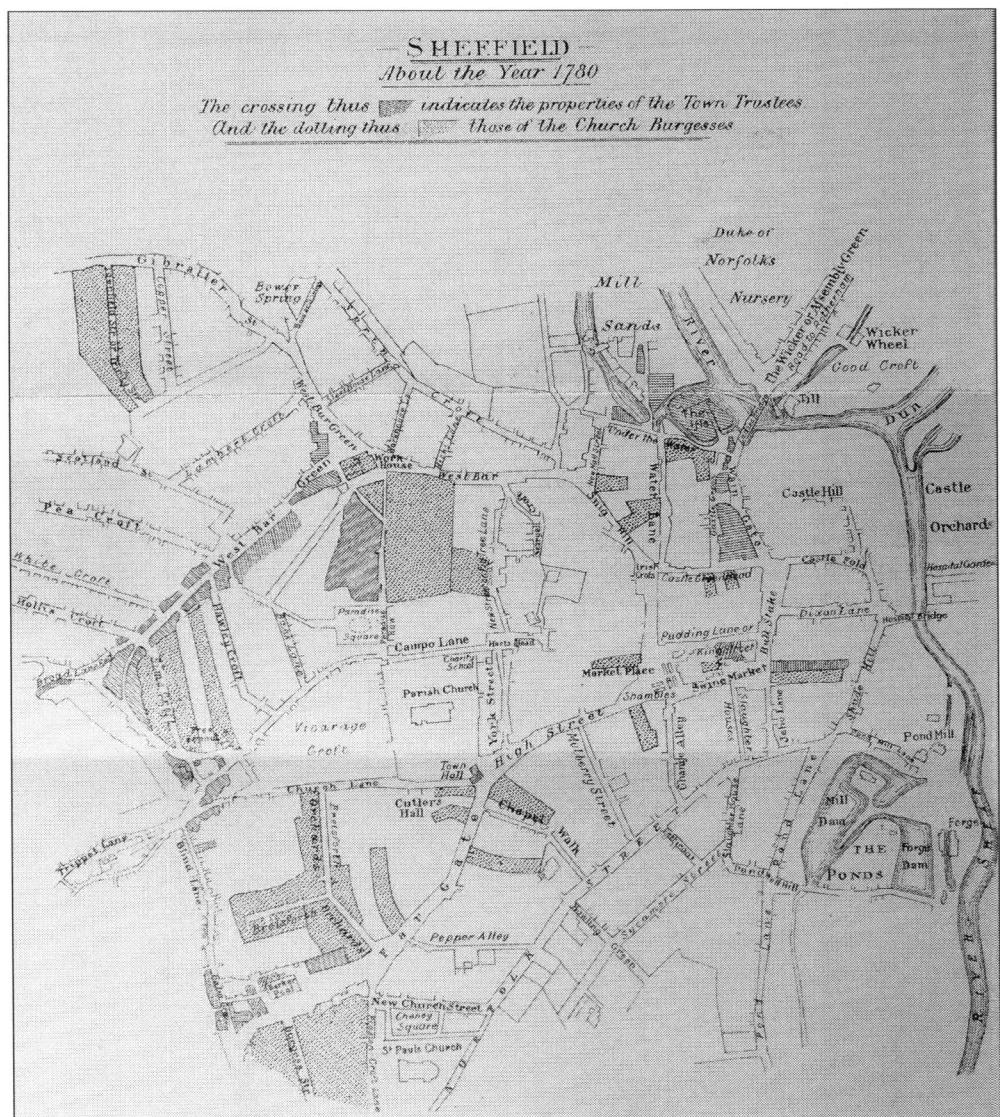

Map of Sheffield (1780) indicating properties owned by Town Trustees.

the clothes that the paupers would wear to distinguish them from the other 'respectable poor people' of the town, and it was agreed the same year that:

For 79 yards of blewish cloth for the appareling of 20ty poore children
    put into the workhouse, £8 18s 5d
For 5 yards and a quarter of white cotton for making 20ty cotes, £1 1s 0d
For 98 yards of hardened [course] cloth, £3 13s 10d
For making the same into 40 smocks for said children, 6s 0d

[P. 23.] Item, paid to Johne Bullas for Leadinge ij Loades of Tymber from Skargell Clause at Brightsyde for mendinge of the Ladye Brydge - - - - - iij s. iiij d.
Item, paid for breade and ale for the Burgesses tennantes for bayring of Tymber to the Brydge ij severall tymes - - - xx d.
Item, given to poore Oates wife, wyddowe, beinge verye sycke and almost famyshed for lacke of foode to her selfe and her children - - - - - - xvj d.

Burgery accounts for 'Oates wife'.

	li.	s.	d.
To Stone (the waite) for his cote - - -	1	0	0
for the dinners of those that were present att the takeing of the last accompt - -	0	10	0
for sweepeing the Bridge and the pauement att the Church yates - - - -	0	7	0
for the dinners of thassembly quest and writing and deliuering in their verdict - -	0	13	6
for Repairing the Buttes in the wicker -	0	3	0
for Repairing the Ladies Bridge - -	4	17	0
for Repairing Barkers poole - - -	1	6	8
for Rent for the woorkhouse croft - -	0	10	0
Delivered to the Overseers of the poore -	13	6	8
for Repairing the woorkhouse - - -	5	9	6
for 22 Muskettes and charges of the cariage of them[1] - - - - - - -	21	15	7
To the Bedle - - - - - -	0	1	0
To the Bellman - - - - -	0	2	0
for writing this accompt - - - -	0	2	6
The Collectours fee - - - - -	0	2	6
the Summe disbursed - -	50	6	11

[1] The purchase of muskets marks the preparation for civil war. Charles I. set up his standard at Nottingham, 22 Aug., 1642.

Burgery Accounts for repairs to butts on the Wicker.

	li.	s.	d.
to James Bright for leading of stone - -	3	6	8
to Richard Shemeld for lattes, nayles and lead -	2	19	6
for 79 yardes of blewish cloth for thapparelling of 20ty poore children putt into the woorkehouse - - - - - - -	8	18	5
for 5 yardes and a quarter of white Cotton -	0	3	6
for makeing 20ty cotes - - - -	1	1	0
for 98 yardes of harden cloth[3] - - -	3	13	10
for makeing the same into 40 smockes for the said children - - - - -	0	6	8
for a cowe giuen to the master of the children -	3	12	4
for 4 nattes[4] for their beddes - - -	0	1	2
Nicholas Parkin on first of May last for his monethes paie before hand of the 10 li. hee is to have with the children - - -	0	16	8
for 65 foote of glasse and 3 casements of glasse-	1	9	6
For the charges and which was given to John Pendleton, who came to have beene a Master			

Burgery Accounts 'for blewish cloth' to make clothes for the workhouse children.

144	BURGERY ACCOUNTS.		[1642.

	li.	s.	d.
the sum disbursed and areare is - -	36	19	11
So Resteth which was delivered to Edward Wood appointed Collector for the next year.	35	0	6

ANNO DOMINI 1642.

[P. 149.] The Burgerie of Sheffeld.—The Accompt of Edward Wood (Collector) there taken the xvj th daie of June 1642 for the Rentes and Revenues belonging to the said Burgerie for one whole year ended att Martinmas last.

The Charge.

	li.	s.	d.
First the said Collector is to be charged with money remeining the Last Reckoning - -	35	0	6
and with a whole yeares Rent ended at Martinmas last - - - - -	20	3	0
and with Rent made of the woorkhouse croft -	1	4	0
and with interest money receiued for 200 li. -	13	6	8
and with arrereages as appeareth att the foote of the last reckoning - - - -	18	13	7
and with parte of Thomas Robertes arrereages	0	6	0
the Summe of the Charge -	88	13	9

Burgery Accounts indicating the workhouse rent of £1 4s.

It is more than likely that there were just children in this early workhouse, as we know that Schools of Industry had been established in many towns by this time. Certainly it was felt that if children of the poor were to be taught the basics of reading and writing they would more easily find employment and would therefore not become a future burden on the ratepayer. The inhabitants of this workhouse were taught to knit by a man who came from Chapel en le Frith in 1633, for which he was paid 3s 4d, and costs of 2s 7d was given to two men from Wakefield 'to have sett the children on work' in 1638.

The workhouse must have been kept in a good state of repair, as there are several entries regarding the maintenance of the building. It seems that the roof was covered with moss rather than thatch in 1635. Timber was supplied for 'laying the long chamber floor' in 1637. Part of the floor was also made up of paving slabs in 1640; a table was also provided. Windows were now filled with glass, hedging was put around the workhouse croft and a gate installed 'with a lock provided for same'. The accounts of 1642 show that the rent for the workhouse was £1 4s. By 1652, the well had a wall built around it by Thomas and Ralph Shore, and two bay windows were slated. There is even listed 6d for a drink given to the workmen. By 1660 there were some spare rooms at the workhouse which were rented out by the workhouse master to Thomas Rawson, who paid 6s 8d a year, and John Crookes, who three years later rented a room at 10s a year. These small entries are absolutely fascinating, and give researchers a tiny window into the building and maintenance of these early workhouses. During those years not all poor people went into the workhouse, as it was noted that in May 1697 the number of persons claiming relief was already 760. A meeting was called on the 5 May of that year to establish the assessment of rates which was to be made for the use of the overseers and churchwardens 'for the poor of ye towne of Sheffield'. It was recorded that the total out-relief which had been paid out that year amounted to £177 17s 10d.

It is not clear when the first workhouse was built in Sheffield, but around 1720 there is a document outlining workhouse rules. The workhouse was governed by two unnamed Overseers of the Poor with churchwardens to assist them in their task or any other person 'if needs require them'. One of the overseers was in charge of buying provisions for the house and every purchase was logged in a book. People of the parish were encouraged to make an appointment with the master to check the log book whenever they required. They were also encouraged to attend meetings held at the house every Friday 'in a manner proper for them to consult the town's business and the poor'. The workhouse rules were also listed:

No one member of a family can enter the workhouse, but all the family must enter. They must bring all their possessions into the workhouse and when they leave their property will be returned to them.

The master will put them to work at 6 a.m. and they will finish work at 6 p.m.

The inmates are allowed half an hour to eat their breakfast and an hour for lunch. Supper is held at 6 p.m. followed by prayers with the master or one of his family, 'the same as in church on Sunday'.

When the inmates attend church on Sunday the master and his wife will walk at the front of the paupers who will follow behind in twos, men first, then the women and children. When a pauper dies the same procession follows the coffin, the master and his wife preceding the remains.

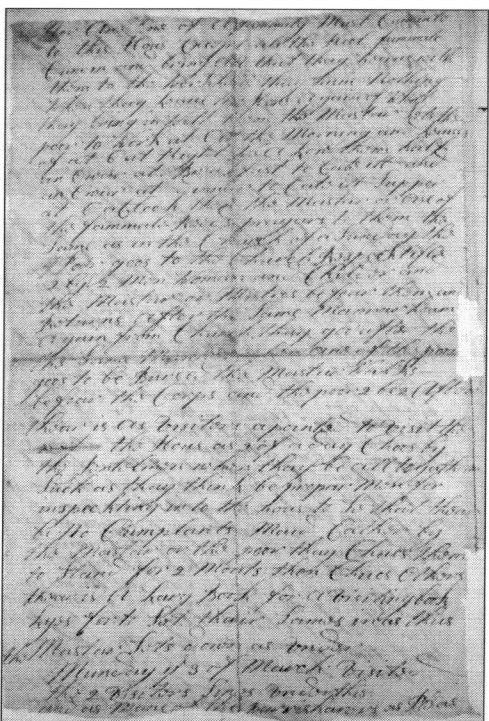

Rules of the early workhouse, thought to date from 1720.

The basic diet for the inmates of the workhouse in 1720.

The meals consisted of:

Sunday
Boiled Milk
Broth & meats & beer
Broth only

Monday
Milk
Boiled puddings & beer
Bread, cheese & beer

Tuesday
Milk
Broth & meat & beer
Broth only

Wednesday
Milk
Boiled pudding & beer
Bread, cheese and beer

Thursday
Milk
Boiled pudding & beer
Bread, cheese and beer

Friday
Milk
Broth & meat & beer
Broth only

Saturday
Milk
Boiled pudding & beer
Bread, cheese & beer

The Workhouse Test Act of 1723 reinforced the idea that anyone seeking help in the workhouse would have to do some work to pay for their stay in the house. Following the Act, a new workhouse, called 'the House of Maintenance for the Poor', was opened in Sheffield in 1733 and the barest details we have of the daily life of the paupers are in the lists of supplies delivered. The cost of coals to the house up to 10 August was £8 12s 6d, and there were seventy-six 'loads of corn' costing £33 8s 8d. During Christmas week the rules seemed to have been relaxed somewhat, and twelve quarts of malt, costing £14 1s, were paid. At that time there were nineteen persons resident in the house, and the week's list of supplies were:

Beer: 3s 6d	Bread: 6s 9d	Baking: 4½d	Cheese: 3s
Coals: 2s 6d	Flour: 3s 9d	Meat: 7s 6d	Milk: 2s
Salt: 3d	Shop goods: 3s 4¾d	Odds: 3s 6¾d	

The total cost was £1 16s 7d, and the master estimated that the cost of relief was 2s 3d per head per week. By 1736 there were twenty-four inmates – consisting of nine men, seven women and eight children – in the house. It seems that the work which was done in the workhouse was mainly sewing. This would have been done by women, and possibly by some of the children, as we see from the records that the women were provided with pins, needles and linen cloth. The men would have been given tasks like stone-breaking or oakum-picking, although they could have been involved in pig-rearing too: two pigs, costing 10s, were bought the same year. Every May the number of paupers in the house was listed, and even from this time the numbers increased from year to year, giving an indication of the overcrowding to come: the number of inmates in 1737 was thirty-four; in 1738 there were thirty-five (of which seventeen were reported as being 'badly' in need of relief); in 1742 there were seventy-seven, and in 1745 the total was ninety-four.

Workhouse Lane.

Kelham Street
Workhouse before
demolition in 1947.

This overcrowding continued until it was agreed by the ratepayers that the workhouse should be improved and enlarged in February 1759. By now the numbers of Sheffield paupers had grown to 111, and two years later (when, presumably, the extension had been completed) there were 156 residents on the books. By 1760, even though the numbers had dropped to 108 paupers, discipline was slipping. One of the overseers on his visit to the workhouse wrote that he 'was informed that Anne Pitt and Hannah Clayton had conveyed a linen sheet and three breadths of blue linsey to Mary Woodhouse at ye White Horse in Gregory Row'. For this act both woman were thrown into the 'dark hole' and were later 'whipt'. Perhaps it was to prevent such things happening again that, in 1750, a Testament was bought for recalcitrant paupers. From a map dated 1780 we know that there was a workhouse at the junction between West Bar and West Bar Green, close to Workhouse Lane, the name which still exists today.

The evidence shows that, despite the deterrent nature of the workhouse system, the numbers of Sheffield paupers increased year by year. This is not surprising given the cyclical nature of industrial depression, which affected towns like Sheffield on a regular basis. Whatever the reason, the matter became so serious that a public meeting was held in 1791 to find a solution. A letter written by the vicar of Sheffield, Mr James Wilkinson, had been printed in the local newspaper regarding the necessity for a new workhouse building. A meeting was called on 6 April 1791: the ratepayers of Sheffield who attended were asked to 'assent or dissent' to the erection of a new workhouse, and permission to borrow the money for it to be built was requested. However, not for the first time – or the last – it was resolved 'that all further proceedings for the erection of a new workhouse be abandoned'. There is no reason given for this decision, but we do know that in Sheffield in 1796 a children's School of Industry was proposed and that it had been estimated that the goods produced by the children's efforts were to be sold to offset the costs. The children would need to work very hard indeed, as by 1798 the rates collected amounted to a staggering £9,009 17s, whilst the costs given out in relief amounted to £8,685 2s 7d. Matters did not improve in the town by January 1801, and once again a public meeting was called to consider the distress being experienced by much of the population due to the high price of provisions. It was reported that 2,000 people attended the meeting to address the 'absolute necessity' that a new workhouse was built for 'the future comfort, accommodation and employment of the poor'. To hold such a crowd, the meeting was, at first, held in a field in the park. However, no conclusions could be reached, and feelings ran so high in the town that the meeting was followed by riots and scenes of violence. Part of the frustration was due to the fact that high numbers of people were out of work and suffering from great poverty, and the natural reluctance to spend more of the ratepayer's money when enlargements of the existing workhouse might possibly solve the problem.

By April 1804 the costs of relief had risen yet again, and it was reported in the *Sheffield Local Register*, printed for John Thomas and sold by Robert Leader, and in the *Sheffield*

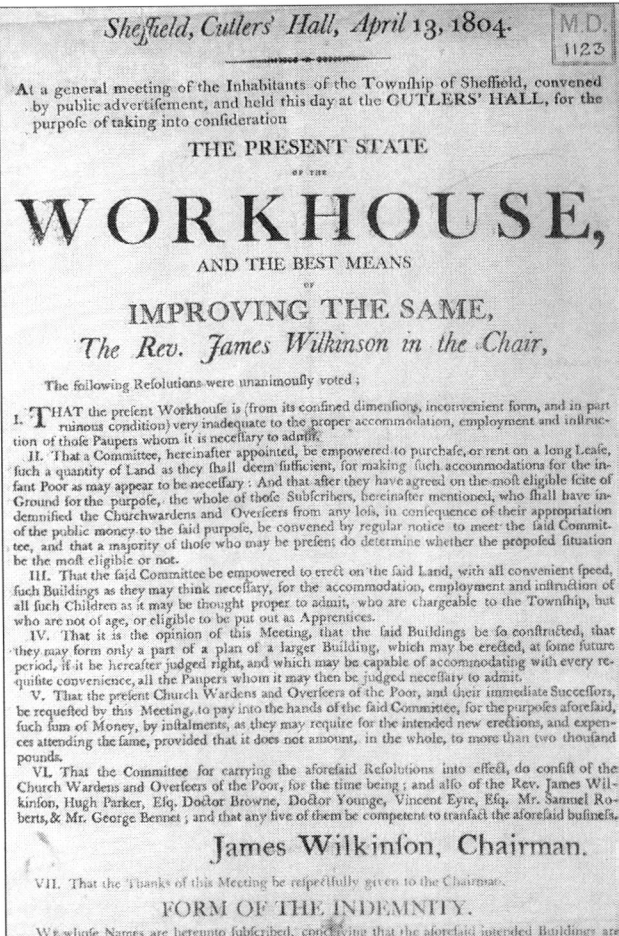

Meeting held on 13 April 1804 agreeing to appoint a committee.

Independent of 1830 that the rates collected had amounted to £12,589 0s 6d, whilst the costs of relief were £12,344 14s 0d. These were enormous amounts of money. There is no more mention of a workhouse until January 1813, when the overseers announced that the costs of relief were now exceeding the amount of rates collected. A committee of fifty-two people were appointed once again to look into the matter. They found, to their disgust, that despite the high levels of relief the overseers were not only paying themselves a salary but had appointed a surveyor. On 7 June 1813, at another public meeting, it was resolved that:

> this meeting highly disapproves of the conduct of the overseers of 1810/11 in having taken the liberty and incurring the enormous expense of appointing surveyors to assess a new rate as well as the overseers of 1812 having added to the expenses of the workhouse by additional salaries without the sanction or authority of a town meeting.

Added to the high feelings on the matter of the erection of a new workhouse, it should be added that the rates were very unpopular amongst the ratepayers. In September of 1820 there were 327 summons issued for non-payment of the poor rates By 1831, out of a population of 59,011 people, there were 4,573 houses with an annual rent of £10 which could be assessed for poor rate. It was obvious at this point that something had to be done. In January 1821, the *Sheffield Mercury* recorded that: 'we believe that this week a number of townspeople will meet the Overseers of the Poor in the course of the ensuing week to take into consideration the propriety of taking any further steps relative to the cotton mill'.

This was the cotton mill on Kelham Street, the purchase of which was at that time deemed necessary to accommodate the large numbers on relief. Once again, however, nothing was resolved, although at some point the overseers rented part of the mill to accommodate a number of paupers. Despite this extra space, the numbers of paupers swelled to the point that it was decided that the workhouse on West Bar was totally inadequate. The urgent need to separate the children from the adult paupers was discussed as early as 13 April 1804 at a public meeting in the Cutlers Hall, where plans were made for a separate workhouse for children. The resolutions from the meeting were printed on a poster, accompanied by 210 signatures of prominent men of the town. They stipulated that:

> The present workhouse is very inadequate for the proper accommodation, employment and instruction of paupers being in part ruinous for the condition of paupers who it is necessary to admit.
>
> That a committee hereafter being appointed be empowered to purchase or rent on a long lease such a quantity of land as they shall deem sufficient for making such accommodation for the infant poor as they may deem necessary. Once they agree on a site they meet regularly and the majority of those present determine whether the proposed situation be the most suitable or not.
>
> The proposed committee is empowered to erect on the said land such buildings as they think necessary for the accommodation, employment and instruction of all such children who are not eligible or of an age to be put out as apprentices'.
>
> That this building be part of a plan to erect larger buildings at a future site which might be capable of accommodating all paupers necessary to admit.

The present churchwarden and overseers are required by this meeting to pay into the hands of the said committee such sums of money by instalments as they may require for the intended new workhouse, providing it does not amount to more than £2,000.

The committee consists of churchwardens, overseers, Revd James Wilkinson, Hugh Parker Esq, Dr Browne, Dr Younge, Vincent Eyre, Samuel Roberts and Mr George Bennett. (*Listing Resolutions at the General Meeting held on April 13th 1804. Ref No. MD1123*)

Not for the first time, there was some dissention amongst the committee, who had been looking for several weeks before they found a site at the top of Lead Mill Fields. Dr John Browne argued that it was too near the centre of town and would soon be surrounded by buildings where 'smoke would be injurious to old and asthmatic people' (*Remarks for the Best Site for the Sheffield Workhouse* May 5th 1804. Ref No. 6296/L7-1). It would seem that at this point the committee was looking for the site of a workhouse which would not exclusively be for children. Samuel Roberts, on the other hand, pointed out that two new wings could be erected on the present workhouse on Westbar 'to accommodate all the in-paupers with decency and comfort' (*Answer to Above by Samuel Roberts*, May 5th 1804. Ref No. 6296/L7-2). Eventually, it was reported that the best situation for the new workhouse was near to Water Lane, which is somewhere beneath the site of the South Yorkshire Police Headquarters of today.

However, there is no further evidence in the records to tell us whether this new workhouse was built, or if Samuel Roberts' suggestion was taken up instead. We do know that on 27 January 1821 there was the first mention in the *Sheffield Directory* of a meeting of ratepayers to consider the purchase of the cotton mill 'lately occupied by Messrs Heathfield

The 210 signatures attached to the notice.

and converting it to a poorhouse'. But it seems that the sale did not go through. The reason could have been an upswing in trade, as it was reported in the *Sheffield Independent* of 18 October 1823 that the smallest sum (£15 9s 9d) had been paid out in one week to the paupers 'within the recollection of the oldest ratepayer'. On 4 August 1828, once again, a public meeting was called by the churchwardens and overseers to decide whether the 'present workhouse on West Bar should be abandoned and the cotton mill fitted up for the reception of the poor'. One of the master cutler's, named Samuel Hadfield, took the chair, and explained to the assembled crowd that the present workhouse was insufficient for the amount of paupers within it. It was not just the accommodation: meals for 300 paupers were cooked in a tiny kitchen of only 9¾ yards by 4½ yards, and one of the lodging rooms, measuring just 5½ yards by 10 yards, contained nine beds. Due to the lack of space it was impossible to classify (separate) all the types of paupers. Residents were therefore

VESTRY MEETING.

THE present WORKHOUSE for the TOWNSHIP of SHEFFIELD being found insufficient, and inconvenient for the accommodation of the Paupers and the other purposes of the Poor, the Churchwardens and Overseers of the Poor of the said Township,

DO HEREBY GIVE NOTICE,

That a VESTRY MEETING of the Inhabitants of the said Township will be held at the Town Hall, in Sheffield aforesaid, on MONDAY, the 4th day of AUGUST, 1828, at eleven o'clock in the Forenoon, to consider of the propriety of erecting and building in such Township a suitable Workhouse; or of altering and enlarging any Messuage or Tenement belonging to such Township for that purpose, and of purchasing or taking on Lease any Ground within the said Township for the purpose of such Building; or of enlarging any such other Messuage or Tenement belonging to such Township for that purpose, or of adding to and enlarging the present Workhouse. Also to consider of the mode of raising money to carry into effect any Resolutions relative to the matters aforesaid, which may at such Meeting be agreed upon; also to assent to or dissent from the sale and disposal of the present Workhouse; and generally, to adopt any Resolutions which may then be thought fit, and proper within the powers or provisions in these respects of the existing Laws; and particularly of an Act of parliament, passed in the 59th year of the late King's Reign, entitled "an Act to amend the Laws for the Relief of the Poor." Dated this 23rd day of July, 1828.

FRANCIS CLULEY
T. N. BARDWELL
JOHN BROWN.
WILLIAM SWIFT.
THOMAS CRESWICK.
NATHANIEL GREAVES.

☞ The Churchwardens and Overseers are prepared with some Proposals, Plans, and Estimates, respecting the purchase of the Cotton Mill, lately occupied by Messrs. Heathfield, and the conversion of it into a Workhouse. These are deposited at the present Workhouse, and may be inspected by the Rate-payers at any time, between now and the proposed Meeting.

Notice for the Public Meeting, 4 August 1828.

forced to share rooms with 'idiots' and other 'characters that ought not to be assembled promiscuously together'. It was resolved that 'the present workhouse on West Bar should be abandoned, the materials sold and the cotton mill formerly owned by Messrs Heathfield and Sons should be purchased'.

The ratepayers of the town were invited to see two sets of plans which had been drawn up by Messrs Watson, Pritchett and Watson of York, plans for both the erection of a new workhouse or for the alterations needed for the cotton mill on Kelham Street (which covered 38,178 square yards and had been offered for sale at the sum of £7,500). These plans were left at the existing workhouse for people to see. Ratepayers were invited to make themselves acquainted with the present state of the workhouse, where the newspaper reported 'they will see the necessity of something being done and that immediately'. A further report stated that the overcrowding at the existing workhouse on West Bar was making things very difficult:

In cases of fever the whole establishment is at risk of contagion... We have heard of a lunatic placed in a ward with twenty or thirty poor aged people who have been compelled in consequence to pass their sleepless nights in a state of alarm. The workhouse shelters aged, diseased and undeserved poverty and though undoubtedly vice and idleness are every day seen within its walls, it will be admitted of all persons of feelings that the unfortunate or incapable should not be subject to inconvenience arising from such a simple cause as want of space for proper habitation.

Part of the driving factor to secure the mill quickly was the fear was that if the mill was sold to new owners the overseers would have to find somewhere else to shelter the overspill from the workhouse proper. It was costing somewhere in the region of £100 per year for this branch of the workhouse and, as they pointed out, this amount would be saved if the ratepayers agreed to the sale. The sale was finally agreed and the owners of the mill were happy for the money to be paid in instalments (£1,000 per year for seven and a half years). We know that by 18 June 1829 the inmates of the workhouse on West Bar were removed to the new workhouse on Kelham Street. To celebrate, it was recorded that the inmates were treated to a meal consisting of 280lbs of meat and 320lbs of pudding, which was served to 317 persons. The previous month, on 5 April 1829, it had been resolved that the materials of the old workhouse were to be sold off by auction, and by 18 August the overseers were advertising the site of the old workhouse (which had now been divided into building lots and disposed of by auction). The produce of this sale realized £970, which was paid into the overseers' accounts. Finally, after much discussion and many arguments, Sheffield had its new workhouse on Kelham Street, which could now accommodate 600 paupers. The maintenance and administration of the workhouse was now run by a group of men known as 'the Overseers of the Poor'.

two

Overseers and Relieving Officers

The Poor Law Act of 1601 ordered that every year two or three respectable men be elected as Overseers of the Poor of the town under the direction of the churchwardens. The elections were held at vestry meetings (in the vestry of churches). These elected men had the responsibility of collecting rates, giving relief to the poor and dealing with apprenticeships for children. For much of the following I am indebted to *The List of Overseers of Sheffield 1608-1787,* which outlines the kind of work which would be done by these men. The list also gives the names of the overseers and the years of their appointments, which include:

1584: Edward Williamson
1585: William Swift
1586: John Hyley
1587: Edmund Swift
1588: John Brighton
1589: Addam Binney
1590: Simon Heathrols
1591: John Smith
1592: George Burnell
1593: Hugh Shalner

All paupers wanting relief had to prove a right of settlement (that is, that they belonged to the town and had a right to live or 'settle' in that parish). Settlement could only be proven if you were born in the town, if a woman married someone from that town, or if you owned a property of a rateable value of £10 within that parish. Where possible, settlement cases were investigated, and relief could be given to all who could prove that they belonged to Sheffield. If a person were taken ill or claimed relief in another township then relief could be paid to them on the understanding that the place of their birth would reimburse the costs. Once the person had recovered they would be returned back to their own parish on an Order of Removal. One of the earliest records within these lists is the removing of a couple who were residents in another district. On 7 May 1717, a pauper named Edward

Dale and his wife were removed by John Coust and George Balmforth, two overseers from Sheffield, to Handsworth and delivered into the hands of the overseer for that district, Mr Baines. The Order for Removal had been signed by two of the churchwardens, Mr Battye and Mr Woodyear, Esq. Both these men would have been upstanding men of the parish and would have been elected into the role of churchwarden in a *ex offio* manner, that is elected automatically due to their status in the community. Many settlement claims were given certificates, as the following example from 1712 shows. It states:

> We the churchwardens and Overseers of the Poor of the town of Sheffield in the County of Yorkshire own and acknowledge William Dickinson, a cutler with his wife and three children to whomever he shall become chargeable unto. Not having elsewhere obtained a legal settlement. Whereof we have hereunto for our hands and sealed the 14th April 1712.

The document was signed by James Watson, Joseph Turner, John Turner and Robert Bridges, and attested by Anthony Heith and Cornelius Dale, who would have been overseers or churchwardens. Another certificate of settlement was given in 1791 to a family which reads as follows:

> James Oates (taylor), Sarah his wife and Sarah and Samuel Oates their children. Their certificate signed 4th March 1791 by Richard Dodson and Joseph Bingham churchwardens and Joseph Turner overseer of the poor certify the said James Oates, Sarah his wife are inhabitants legally settled in Handsworth aforesaid.

However, some of these certificates were found to be fraudulent. On 20 January 1730, it was discovered that:

> the granting of certificates to some persons in the township of Attercliffe cum Darnall have been found to be of pernicious consequences. It is therefore agreed by the township on the date above written that the chapel wardens and Overseers of the Poor or either of them shall not sign any certificate but at a public town meeting where the heads of both towns or such others of the inhabitants are there and can give an account of the person and share reasons why it may or may not be convenient that such certificates shall be granted. (List of Overseers of Sheffield 1608–1787. Ref. No. CA26/1)

When workhouses were first established, the procedure was that any poor persons who needed help would generally have first approached the overseer to request relief or admittance to the workhouse. Those who went directly to the workhouse would meet the master who would make arrangements for them to be questioned by the overseers. The overseers would take details of name, age and the date of the month the claimant first entered the house. The rules stated that 'all paupers are obliged to stay in the workhouse for a full 12 months and not to go out of the house in summer and come in again in winter, but stay until the same time of year they came in' (*Rules of the Workhouse in Sheffield*, reference No. CA24/57).

In November 1811 there was such a shortage of coins that the Overseers of the Poor were given permission to make their own tokens which were given in the form of out-relief. The tokens, which were made of silver, were not to exceed £10,000 in 1s and 2s currency. Other firms were anxious to copy this, and some gold and silver tokens were issued by Messrs Young, Wilson and Young. However, it was pointed out that coining like this was illegal and Young, Wilson and Young's coins were withdrawn from circulation on 16 August 1812. Only Sheffield workhouse's authorities could make their own coins. The practice was discontinued when more coins became available, but after another public meeting on 4 December 1814 it was resolved that the overseers should once more be authorised to use the silver tokens issued by their predecessors. The same coins were used again on 1 July 1842, during a period of industrial depression. The economic conditions were horrific, so much so that James Montgomery Esq. stated: 'the oldest inhabitants of Sheffield cannot remember a crisis of calamity so apparently hopeless as that which has come upon us. The labouring classes have been going down into abject destitution'.

When the Poor Law Amendment Act of 1834 was established, the Guardians of the Kelham Street workhouse appointed relieving officers. These were then paid a salary. We do not have a list of these early relieving officers, but a later one, from Fir Vale in June 1890, still exists. Their work was complementary to the overseers, who were still responsible for making provision in bastardy cases and licensing issues within the town. The relieving officers had a room in the workhouse to pay out-relief and to listen to applications as well as stations or rooms throughout the districts. It was the duty of the relieving officers to make house visits in the case of sickness and to issue orders for the Medical Officers to attend to the sick paupers living outside of the workhouse. He had his own books in which he kept all his accounts. These had to be presented to the Guardians and checked by the clerk before every Board meeting. He also had to undertake any other tasks as appointed by the Guardians.

When stationed at the parishes, the relieving officers would listen to the claims of persons asking to enter the workhouse and he would be given an order for the house whilst the claim was checked. Sometimes paupers were sent straight to the workhouse from the police station at the Town Hall. We have a note copied into the letter book of the Sheffield Guardians in September 1847, regarding an unknown woman sent into the workhouse by the relieving officer Mr Wilkinson. The note is addressed to Mr Rogers and reads: 'Mr Wilkinson begs to recommend the case of the bearer to the consideration of Mr Rogers. Mr Wilkinson having known her for many years as a very industrious and honest woman and he thinks she had better be taken into the house.'

Workhouse tokens, used as money.

Another very sad referral is made by one of the relieving officers for Brightside. Mr W. Bruce sent an old woman called Ann Shaw into the Kelham Street workhouse. She was described as a widow who had lived in a court in Marcus Street with her son and his wife (who had recently given birth). Her son was dangerously ill and it was not felt that he would get better. Mrs Shaw had taken care of herself and her son's family by taking in washing, and she had 'never in her life applied for or had parish relief'. He told Mr Rogers that, 'I shall feel much obliged if you will allow it to be attended to'.

When children were sent to the workhouse after being deserted by their parents, it was the relieving officer's role to try to apprehend the parents and force them to pay for the cost of relief of their children in the workhouse. Claims were rigorously investigated, but some parents escaped having to pay the maintenance for their relative in the workhouse – for a few years at least. On 12 January 1848, a letter marked 'urgent' was sent to Mr Rogers from Jane Catherine Richards of High Street, Uttoxeter. Mrs Richards had heard that a little girl of eleven years of age was at that time in the Kelham Street workhouse; she estimated that the girl had been in the workhouse for two years and said that her name was Cornelia King or Kelly – or perhaps she might have been left under the name of Webster? She requested an answer by return of post, writing, 'I believe I can inform you where the girl's legal father can be found who is well able to maintain a child without her being left to be maintained on a parish where funds are heavy enough'. The master immediately replied that the girl was indeed in the house, and he received a reply on 14 January which I include in full. She wrote:

I have to inform you that a man of the name of John Richardson Kelly came to this town and took a business of printer, bookseller and stationer in 1844. In the summer of 1847 he had a journeyman working for him who he told a secret that his master had another wife in Yorkshire. He said that his master had been married in the assumed name of King to an Elizabeth Lister at Whitby in Yorkshire in February 1834 who he afterwards deserted at Doncaster. He left her with a child who was now in Sheffield workhouse. Kelly was again married to a young woman in the town in September of 1840. The tale was frequently spoken about in private and many wondered if it was true. Nothing further was known for certain until October last when a gentleman wrote to the parish clerk at Whitby and obtained a certificate of the marriage and sent it to Mr Richards [her husband]. Mr Richards was perfectly astounded to find that there was real truth attached to this report and he has since been in correspondence with Kelly's first wife and it is from her that we have heard where the child is. Mr Kelly is still in the business which reports say is a good one. Any more information you may wish I will give you or anyone else you may appoint to make enquiries.

The relieving officers proceeded to Uttoxeter where Mr Kelly was found and brought back to Sheffield. He was proceeded against for maintenance for his wife and his daughter. The master wrote to Mrs Kelly requesting that she comes to Sheffield, and warning her that 'though it may not be desirable for you to anticipate a renewal of conjugal rights' that her husband would indeed be liable for payments for her support. This intriguing tale leaves unanswered the reason why a child was put into the workhouse whilst her mother lived elsewhere. If Mrs Kelly was able to receive support from her errant husband, was she able to keep the little girl with her? We may never know.

The relieving officers would be well aware that the costs of relief in the town of Sheffield were rising year by year. On 24 September 1851, when the workhouse at Kelham Street had been open for twenty-two years, Mr Farnall, the Poor Law Inspector, visited the workhouse and told the overseers and the relieving officers that the average cost of paupers in the Sheffield workhouse was the highest of all the neighbouring towns. He told them that the average cost per head for the paupers of Sheffield was £4 8s 2¼d per year, whilst the average of the rest of his district was £3 5s 3½d, and he urged both the Guardians and the relieving officers to be more diligent when making enquiries into claims for relief. Matters did not improve, however, and he visited the workhouse again on the morning of Thursday, 18 September 1856. In the morning he examined all the workhouse books, and in the afternoon he addressed the Guardians and told them once again – and in no uncertain terms – that the costs of relief at Sheffield were too high. He informed them that he had found numbers of able-bodied young men in the workhouse, stating that:

> I must lay before you the facts and figures as it is my duty. There is no union or township in my district that occupies such an unfortunate position as Sheffield. You have 1,948 old people on relief, 202 of which are resident in the workhouse and the rest are on out-relief. There are 230 children who we must educate and 28 able bodied paupers in the house and 1,108 more on outdoor relief and it is to these that you must address your attention. There may be women with illegitimate children much to the dissatisfaction of society at large. To give relief unnecessarily to able-bodied poor is the most cruel proceedings of which you are guilty.

It seems very much that the relieving officers were in a dilemma: if they refused relief and that person died they would have to take full responsibility, but they were also aware that there were men in the workhouse who simply refused to work. The *Sheffield Daily Telegraph* on Wednesday, 25 September 1865 reported that two able-bodied young men had been brought before the Guardians at the Board meeting that day. The paper described the first young man as being perfectly fit and 'labouring under no physical defect'. He was named as William Skinner, aged twenty-one, who had previously been a scissor-grinder. Much of his time had been spent in and out of the workhouse. He told the Guardians and overseers that he had been unable to get any work at all, but the Guardians showed no sympathy and ordered his discharge. The second young man came in and gave his name as William Ford. He was twenty-five years of age, and was 'tall, stout and fresh looking'. The chair addressed him: 'Well, Ford, can't you get any work?' 'No, sir,' he replied. 'I have tried and tried. I've neither father nor mother to do owt for me.' But the Guardians were relentless, and discharged him also. The relieving officers reported back the following week and revealed that both men were back in the workhouse: they had no option but to allow them to return. There was nothing the Guardians could do about this: they appealed to the Poor Law Commissioners for any help or advice they could give, but they were afraid that if relief were denied and the applicant died it would be the Guardians' and relieving officers' responsibility.

Letter from Mr Wilkinson to Master Samuel Rogers regarding an unnamed pauper.

Letter from Mr Bruce to Samuel Rogers regarding Ann Shaw.

Letter from Mrs Richards of Uttoxeter regarding Cornelia King.

AN OLD COUPLE'S
QUARTERS.

An elderly couple's quarters, found at
workhouses up and down the country.

Despite their diligence, there were still cases of fraudulent claims which came to the attention of the Guardians. At a meeting on 14 January 1857, the Guardians discussed several cases which had recently come to light. One involved an alleged pauper named Hannah Mettam of Ranmoor, who had been at the workhouse claiming relief that very morning. When one of the Guardians, Mr Mitchell, entered the room where the relief was being paid he realised that he recognised her — and that she had £180 worth of shares in the Sheffield Banking Co. He challenged her about it, and she told him that she was unable to claim her dividends until the following week and that, until that time, she was quite destitute. Mr Mitchell told her to be on her way, and her claims were dismissed. He told the other Guardians that he feared that this was not a solitary case, and that he understood that there were many more cases of fraud. Another Guardian, Mr Peel, agreed, and said he was aware of another case which had been discovered of a woman having savings who had been allowed 3s a week by the relieving officer. Although there is no doubt that the relieving officers carried out their enquiries with much diligence, the frauds continued.

Another curious ambiguity about the workhouse system came to light in January of 1875, when it was stated by the relieving officer, Mr Turnell, that a man had sent his wife into the workhouse — and that 'as he had a good situation [he] was maintaining her there for 5s 3d a week'. One of the Guardians, Mr Spencer, stated that there were other similar cases: often, wives who had been found guilty of adultery were punished by their husbands by being sent to the workhouse. The costs of the women's maintenance were then paid by their cuckolded husbands. Mr Turnell said that there were scores of these cases in the house at present, and that there were, at that time, arrears of £300 from such cases. The Guardians referred the matter to the visiting committee to investigate and to report back to the Board. There is no evidence about what the findings of this committee were, but it was resolved by the Guardians that to try to prevent such occurrences happening again that they insert an advertisement asking people to inform the Guardians of any cases of paupers receiving relief fraudulently.

Sometimes the sheer number of cases was overwhelming for the relieving officers, particularly during times of industrial depression. There had been many complaints in May 1843 from the men who had been forced onto the parish that the scale of work was too much for the cost of relief that they received. They complained to the relieving officer, who asked if a committee of the men could meet the Guardians on 14 May to discuss the situation. The deputation, which had previously held a public meeting in Paradise Square, had voted to go on strike because of the impossible amount of work that faced them. The Guardians agreed to meet with them, and as a result the scale of work was reduced.

Sometimes links with local businesses worked with the Guardians in matters of relief. In January 1858, a letter had been sent from Messrs Mappin Bros enclosing a list of thirty-four men who had been given relief at the workhouse when they were forced to lay them off. Now they had work for them, and asked the relieving officers to send the men back. The Guardians discussed whether it would be practical to print a list of the names of all the men in the house and their trade in the local newspaper where they might be offered a job by local employers, but the chair pointed out that they could not publish the names of paupers on relief. They also discussed visiting the local industries to find out if men were needed, but the idea was abandoned as being too time-consuming. The Guardians by now had several work schemes underway to employ the men on relief. In August 1861, the relieving officers were still finding more cases of men who refused offers of work. They told the Guardians that, due to the depressed state of industry, some workmen were being asked by their employers to work for a lower rate. One of these was a man named James Booker, a single man with no children, who had been asked to work for £1 1s a week. He preferred to go on relief instead, claiming that he was unemployed. The Medical Officer, Mr Skinner, had examined him and reported to the Guardians that he was fit to work, and that 'he was so disgusted that he would have discharged the man at once but he wanted him to be examined by the Board'. The Guardians decided that they could not give relief to men who had work to go to, and upon enquiring how much the man would have earned prior to the distress was told that it was a sum of between £1 5s and £1 10s a week. A Board member commented that it was a pity that the man couldn't be sent to prison, and he was discharged forthwith.

By 13 March 1858 the number of men on outdoor relief was astronomical. The relieving officers informed the Guardians that 370 men were employed on the farms, and another 933 were on relief. Some of those were employed at Deep Pits near Intake levelling earth; others were at Kilton Hill, Occupation Road constructing roads; yet more men were working near to the Manchester, Sheffield and Lincolnshire Railway on land owned by the Duke of Norfolk. The men worked under a superintendent of labour, but it seems that the supervision was lax in the extreme. Another Guardian reported that some of the men supposedly working on the Duke of Norfolk's site had not gone to work and had been working elsewhere whilst still claiming relief. Upon hearing this, one of the Guardians, Mr Crowther, and one of the relieving officers, Mr Wollam, went to the Deep Pit site: there they found that of the 420 men supposedly working on the site, only 80 were actually there. At the next meeting the Guardians agreed that the superintendent should hold a roll call at 8.30 a.m., 12 noon (before the men went home for dinner), at 1.30 p.m. on their return and finally at 4 p.m. when they went home. Anyone who didn't turn up for the roll call would lose half a day's pay. Those who did not turn up for two consecutive days would then have to re-apply for relief in the normal way. A deputation of working men went to see the relieving officers to demand that the Guardians relax the rules. They asked:

- That the superintendent could give the men permission to leave the site to find work
- The roll call only be done in the morning on rainy days
- An extra half hour to be allowed for lunch as some of the men had to walk back to their homes and return for 1.30 p.m.

Mr Wollam told them that any requests would have to be made before the Guardians' meetings. However, on this occasion the Guardians refused to accede to their requests. A few days later, an anonymous letter was received by Mr Crowther containing threats to his life, and also to the life of Mr Wollam. It was immediately put into the hands of the Chief Constable.

When the workhouse was brought under the Poor Law Amendment Act it was decided that the Sheffield area was to be divided into two areas: Sheffield and Brightside would be one area, and Attercliffe would be the other. A relieving officer for each district was appointed in 1838. Twenty years later, as the numbers of Sheffield paupers continued to grow, an assistant relieving officer was appointed. In June 1858 there were three relieving officers: Mr Wollam, whose salary was £150 per year; Mr Hardcastle, paid £140; and Mr Bennett, who was paid £60. The Guardians were fortunate in this appointment, as Mr Bennett proved to be one of the longest-serving relieving officers. He was still working in 1873, but was censored for giving an order for admittance to a young man to the workhouse hospital simply because he was suffering from a loathsome disease (probably syphilis). One of the Guardians, Mr Turnell, contended that a relieving officer had no right to give orders for admission 'except in the most extreme and urgent cases and this case was not of that character'. He pointed out that the relieving officer in question was an old officer and he knew his duties perfectly well. In view of his age and long service, however, the Guardians rebuked him gently for this oversight.

At the Guardians' meeting on 8 November 1865, a complaint was heard against one of the relieving officers, Mr Sykes, who also had held his post for many years. One of the Guardians, Mr Jackson, had received the complaint from a woman, Jemima Collier, who attended the Board meeting and explained that her husband had been out of work for some weeks, and that she had therefore been told by the Medical Officer, Dr Shaw, to apply for relief. However, when she approached Mr Sykes he turned her down, telling her he did not approve of giving relief to twenty-seven-year-old men. Mrs Collier told him that she had two children; she had sold all their garden produce, and now had nothing. They didn't have any food in the house, and her husband 'was dropping for want'. She reminded him that Dr Shaw had told her to apply; 'tell Dr Shaw,' he replied, 'to mind his own business, and I will mind mine.' A second witness, Susannah Wireman, then appeared before the Guardians and affirmed all that Mrs Collier had said. Mr Sykes was invited to give his version of the events. He denied that Mrs Collier had told him that she was in want, and left the Boardroom whilst the Guardians discussed the case. Appallingly, one of them, Mr Hurst, pointed out that Mrs Collier had appeared to be 'respectfully dressed and that a person would not be so dressed that was so poor'. Other Guardians believed that the increase in the population had caused Mr Sykes to increase his duties, and the chair commented that Sykes' age might be making him more irritable. He proposed that he stand down and let a younger man do the job. Mr Hallam thought that the case was not

A typical workhouse admission form.

St. Marylebone Workhouse

Admission by Master

.... order of admission

.... 1901.

Name ....

Age ....

Creed ....

Occupation ....

Single   Married   Widowed

Last Residence ....

....

Whether in W.H. before............

Cause of Admission............

Nearest Relative ....

....

....

PAUPER'S ADMISSION ORDER.

sufficient to ask Mr Sykes to resign. Mr Sykes was brought back into the room and cautioned as to his further treatment of the poor who came to him for relief.

In October 1873 the relieving officers themselves were complaining, this time about the police attitude to the warrants which were taken out to remedy the neglect and desertion by husbands and fathers whose wives were at that time in the workhouse. One of the relieving officers stated that the police were very slow in taking action, and as a result many men were free on the streets of Sheffield whilst the ratepayers were supporting their families. Mr Bennett told the Board that he had issued a warrant for the apprehension of a man named Dalton in May of that year. The warrant came back into his hands three weeks later – at which point the police claimed that the man had 'left the district'. However, Mr Bennett knew that Dalton had not left the district, and caused the man to be apprehended at once. He had been told that Dalton had been in the town all the time; such cases were heard by the relieving officers on a weekly basis. The chair asked the Chief Constable, Mr Jackson, to attend the meeting and he enquired if arrangements could be made for the more speedy execution of summonses and warrants in cases of neglect. The Chief Constable suggested that perhaps the deserted wives could go to the Town Hall and give a description of their husbands, as well as a list of any of his known haunts, to which the Guardians agreed.

By December 1890 the relieving officers were also involved in reporting back to the Guardians on the condition of any cases of children who were boarded out with foster carers. A case was brought before the Guardians the following year from Mr A. Ellis, who had taken a fifteen-year-old girl into his service two months' previously named Clara Billam. Since then, she had admitted that she was pregnant. A relieving officer went to see the girl and she admitted that it was true and he was forced to bring her back to the workhouse. The Guardians were informed of her condition and that her father agreed to pay for her maintenance in the workhouse. The relieving officer, Mr Richards, had also been to see the putative father, a man named Toothill who also had expressed willingness to provide for the girl and the baby in any way that the Guardians felt necessary. However, he pointed out that he was unable to marry her as he was still financially dependent on his own father. The Guardians resolved that the Chief Constable be notified of the case: as the girl was under sixteen, the police could have wished to take out proceedings against the man.

The Chief Constable of Sheffield, Mr John Jackson.

The role of the relieving officer was one of the hardest of all the workhouse positions. They were the ones that saw the poverty and distress of Victorian Sheffield at first hand. Many people would literally starve before they would enter the workhouse, and destitution was chronic during this period. An indication of the miserable lives led by some Sheffield residents outside of the workhouse was printed in the local newspaper on 5 May 1860. An inquest on the body of Mary Morley, wife of Frederick Morley, a furnace man, was held at the Matilda Tavern on 1 May. She had been taken ill, and was unable to leave the house for two or three weeks before she died, aged thirty-eight, leaving one child aged three months old and another two years old. At the end of April 1860 Morley asked a neighbour, a woman named Shaw, to visit his wife. When she did, she found that the woman was almost naked, with just a chemise to cover her. The children were in an equally filthy state. There was nothing in the house to eat apart from some dry bread, and no furniture apart from two chairs and some straw for a bed. Shaw gave her some food, which she ate greedily (even though she was suffering from ulcers in her mouth); she took her some gruel the next morning, and Mrs Morley asked her to stay while she ate it, the implication being that if Shaw left her husband would take the food away. In the presence of the husband, Shaw asked Mrs Morley 'why she was brought so low'. She replied that on Monday her husband would not get her any food at all, though he loudly insisted she was lying. Mrs Morley told another neighbour that he had never beaten her, but he had 'left her with a hungry belly many, many times'. She refused to lie on the straw where her husband slept, but instead sat in the chair all day and night until she finally collapsed on the bare floor – where she died. Both children were removed to the workhouse after her death and were being cared for by workhouse officials.

At the inquest Morley told the coroner that he had given his wife 16s a week for food. The coroner questioned why there was no food in the house: Morley told him that she had not been well enough to go to the market. He asked him why they had not applied for relief or for a Medical Officer to attend to her: he said that he did not want to ask for relief, but instead had sold all the furniture for food.

The husband was then sent out of the room. The coroner asked the police authorities if the man spent his money on drink; he was told that Morley was a teetotaller, but that he 'went with' other woman. When Morley returned to the room the coroner challenged him with this: he denied it. It was also established that he worked for a Mr Bagshaw, who had paid him 27s the first week, 13s the second and 16s the third week, ample enough to have provided nourishment for his wife and children. A post-mortem showed that Mrs Morley had died through inflammation of the brain and left lung, but that death had been hastened by want of proper attention and nourishment. A neighbour, Thomas Guest of Broad Lane, stated that six months ago Morley lived next door to him, and that at that time he regularly starved his wife. The jury brought in a verdict that she had died of debility resulting from inflammation of the lungs and censored the husband for his treatment of her.

Just before the funeral, several hundred people gathered outside Morley's house, waiting for him to come out. When he did, there was loud hooting and booing, which lasted the entire route to the cemetery – a trip Morley made flanked by two constables. On arrival at the cemetery, it was estimated there were between 1,500 to 2,000 persons assembled. The cemetery gates had been locked to keep the crowd out, but the throng burst through the gates and the police were forced to lock Morley in the vestry until the interment was complete. These were the kind of conditions suffered by many poor people in Sheffield, and these were the kind of issues that many of the relieving officers would witness at first hand.

Surprisingly, they were a group that had the least complaints made about them, and they appeared to be a diligent and hardworking group of men. As the numbers of persons on relief increased and the workhouse became bigger a further officer was taken on, and we know that there were four relieving offices by the time that the paupers moved into Kelham Street workhouse.

three

Kelham Street and Fir Vale Workhouses

The workhouse on Kelham Street had been described by one of the Guardians as being situated in the valley of the River Don, the site being desirable as 'the breezes from the river carried away from the workhouse all the noxious vapors from the town and as for ventilation it could not be bettered'. The ex-cotton mill was six-storeys high, and its situation was thought to be far enough away from the centre of the town and all the attendant distractions. The new workhouse was reported to be fireproof due to the stone staircases throughout. In the autumn of 1866, Dr Edward Smith was commissioned by the Poor Law Board to make an inspection of the Kelham Street workhouse and the report was placed before Parliament in January 1868. This report gives us a view of what the inside of this now lost building looked like.

> The rooms are large as befitting a mill but not so convenient for the purpose of a workhouse. There is a detached three-storey Infirmary divided in the middle for the separation of the sexes where there are sick and offensive cases. There are wards at either end of the main wards for the reception of fever and small-pox cases although these were usually locked when not in use. At each end are the male and female lunatic wards with yards attached. At the opposite side is the wards now used for sick children. There are two lying-in wards which are placed near the wards for the aged and sick elderly paupers. There is a verandah of considerable width on each of the floors in front of the Infirmary to enable the patients to have fresh air in a southern aspect. The beds were all made of iron, some having wooden footboards or sides. The mattresses are made of flock or straw and the counterpanes are woollen. There are water closets on each floor and fixed baths for the sick. Personal washing is done in pottery basins and roller towels and hot water is provided.

The opening of the large workhouse was seen as a great success, but before very long, and due to a variety of reasons, the numbers on relief once again began to rise. The workhouse system ultimately failed nationally because the Guardians and the Poor Law authorities had underestimated the large numbers of pauper groups that were unable to be moved on: groups such as mothers with young children, elderly paupers and imbeciles who could

The rear of Kelham Street workhouse before demolition in 1947.

manage little jobs in the workhouse but could never earn a living outside. The town of Sheffield was also liable to massive industrial depressions when the state of trade would decrease and hundreds of men would be out of work. Kelham Street workhouse was enlarged to try and accommodate the hundreds of people on relief. A later photograph, taken just before its demolition in 1947, shows the rear of the Kelham Street workhouse and all the extra sheds at the back which might have been added by the Guardians to relieve the different wards within.

By the 1830s it was not only the town of Sheffield that was suffering from trade depression: the Poor Law system itself was at the point of meltdown. More and more people were being forced to claim relief, and the government decided that something must be done. In 1832 a Royal Commission was asked to look into the Poor Law System to try to find a way of dealing with the large numbers of people claiming relief. The result, as we have seen, was the implementation of the Poor Law Amendment Act and the Poor Law Commission was born. This was a centralized body of men who regulated the system of poor relief throughout England. There was a lot of opposition to the Act in the town of Sheffield and beyond, even though there were regular cases of people starving to death. A letter was sent to the editor of the *Sheffield Iris* on Tuesday, 12 September 1837 by someone signing himself as 'SR', who wrote: 'During the last week there have been two instances of starvation to death so declared by a coroner's jury, which have not been brought to public attention. How many more cases are there? No one can tell and very few care.'

Despite the fact that people were starving to death on the streets of Sheffield, the antagonism towards the introduction of the Act, and particularly towards the Poor Law Commission, was felt throughout Yorkshire. Most towns believed that they should have strategies to deal with their own poor, rather than be told what to do by the three Commissioners based in London. Protest meetings were held in Huddersfield, Bradford and Halifax, and in Sheffield, on 3 May 1837, Paradise Square was crowded with people

The airing yard of a London workhouse: some typical workhouse inmates of the late Victorian era are seen here relaxing, just as they would have done on the 'verandah' at Sheffield.

opposing the Act. Over 16,000 signatures had been obtained to petition Parliament to repeal the Act. However, this opposition was futile and the Act was brought into force nonetheless.

By 9 May 1842 the costs of relief were escalating again due to industrial depression, and the numbers in the workhouse had gone from 200 (in March) to 900 (in May). A meeting was held on 30 August 1842 where it was revealed that 'there are 25,000 inhabited houses [in this parish] and the population of the town consists of 30,000 male adults'. Women and children over twelve accounted for another 7,000. Of these, 4,000–5,000 men were in fulltime work, whose average earnings amounted to 18s a week; about 1,000 men, women and children were only earning 5s a week. Of that number, 17,000 were in part-time employment on an average of 9s a week, and approximately 4,500 women and children were only earning 3s a week. There were 3,000 unemployed men (of which 2,000 were on parish relief) and 1,500 women and children.

It was in the Guardians' interests that the numbers of people on relief were lowered, and several schemes were put into place to save the ratepayers money. One of these was the sending back of Irish paupers who wished to return to Ireland. This scheme was revealed in November 1847 when the Huddersfield Guardians wrote to the master, Mr Rogers, asking about a man named Henry Williams (aged twenty) who had turned up at Huddersfield workhouse wanting them to return him to Ireland after ten days in the fever wards of Kelham Street hospital. The Guardians instructed him to reply; he did, stating that Williams had discharged himself on 25 October. On that day there had been a party of nine paupers who were being sent back to Ireland in the charge of an officer. If Williams had mentioned that his settlement was in Ireland, and that he wanted to return there, the master would have gladly included him in the party. However, he was not listed in the books as being Irish. If he had asked for support or advice, it would have been offered to him.

Occasionally a pauper would be recommended to the Guardians from a local tradesman. A letter was received, dated 28 December 1847, from Henry Atkins of Henry Atkins and Co., makers of silver-plated cutlery based at 32 Howard Street. The letter read:

Dear Sirs, The bearer, Thomas Moor, was once a respectable ratepayer in Sheffield but through a long series of family disasters he is now reduced to seeking the workhouse. He was formerly an accountant and afterwards a schoolmaster until infirmities and his age rendered him incapable of performing his duties efficiently. He has a testimonial from Lord Galway, Rev R. Rogers and others last in connection with him as a parochial schoolmaster. If you can do anything for him I am sure you will as he is utterly destitute.

The massive overcrowding continued. Only twenty-four years after the Kelham Street workhouse opened, the Poor Law Board were once more being critical of the workhouse. On 12 October 1853, the Board advised the Guardians on the propriety of providing a new workhouse for the town of Sheffield. An Inspector of the Poor Law Board had visited the former cotton mill, and stated that:

Because of the original design the wards of the hospital could only be accessed by other rooms and when a pauper died it would involve them being carried through the other rooms on the way to the mortuary. The only water closets, which emptied out into ash pits, were in the yards of the workhouse. The lying-in wards are at the top of the building and again because of the former use are not private in any way for the women giving birth.

The next three floors contained the dormitories. An adjoining building provided the nursery wards for infant children, which were reported to be below the level of the street and consequently damp. All the rooms were described as being 'low, dark and ill ventilated'. The day rooms of the able-bodied men were found in the previous mill house

Letter from Henry Atkins regarding Thomas Moor.

and the rooms above those and the nursery were overcrowded and ill ventilated. The ward occupied by elderly men was offensive and the day rooms occupied by elderly women from the vagrant wards were contaminated by a very offensive smell from the privies.

But the Sheffield Guardians refused to accept that another workhouse was needed, mainly because they knew that the ratepayers of the town were against the idea. By January 1854 the Guardians were informed that 1,228 men, 1,072 women and 945 children had been admitted to the workhouse on Kelham Street. The relieving officer stated that another fifty-seven children had been born in the workhouse, making a total of 3,300 paupers. The Guardians were in a quandary and the chair to the Guardians requested that his colleagues consider the matter urgently in June 1855. When word got out that the Poor Law authorities were insisting on a new workhouse, a meeting of ratepayers was held on 12 November 1855 'to express to the Guardians the sentiment of the crowd which was very much against the new proposed workhouse'. Due to the high numbers of paupers at that time in the workhouse it had certainly become a pressing matter. Finally, the Guardians had no option, and on 14 November 1855 they voted by a majority of eight to three that the present workhouse accommodation was insufficient and a new workhouse should be built. On 26 December the majority of the Guardians signed the order from the Poor Law Board for the building. The Guardians of Sheffield workhouse had no idea what they were about to take on.

There was a further public meeting on 17 March 1856, once again to demonstrate mass opposition to the new workhouse. The ratepayers decided that if the Guardians were in agreement with the Poor Law authorities then they would oppose those Guardians. Two days later there was another meeting, held in the different wards of the town, to discuss the forthcoming election of Guardians, and it was agreed that the public would only vote for those Guardians who were opposed to the building of a new workhouse. The Guardians had resolved to buy a piece of land for the new workhouse, fifty acres in Darnall owned by Mr R. Brashaw, just before the election of the Guardians on 26 March. The Poor Law Board gave their approval on 1 April, but it was already too late. On 11 April all the Guardians that were elected were opposed to the building of the new workhouse, and the number of votes proved how high the feeling in the town against the building was. The newly elected Guardians and their votes were published in the local newspaper, and all the votes, without exception, were double what they had been in previous years. The previous Guardians, as an act of final defiance, sent the Poor Law Board their written consent to the order for the erection of a new workhouse. When the new Board met for the first time they refused to confirm the Minutes of the previous Board, or to instruct the solicitors who had been engaged by their predecessors to do the conveyancing of the land.

However, they did appoint a committee to look into the matter and report back. On 9 June 1856, the Poor Law Board wrote to the new Board of Guardians to enquire what steps had been taken regarding the land at Darnall. They replied that as the appointed committee had not got back to them on the decision they would be in touch as soon as possible. By the 16th, when the Poor Law Board had heard nothing further, they urged the Guardians once again to call on the committee for an urgent decision. The secretary of the committee, a man named Aaron Booth, submitted his report to the Guardians at their meeting on Wednesday, 15 June 1856. It stated quite clearly that:

Upper level of Kelham Street workhouse before demolition in 1947. These were the lying-in wards.

Interior of Kelham Street workhouse before demolition. The large rooms prevented proper classification.

Sheffield Town Hall.

The committee have carefully examined the various proceedings of the late Board relative for the alleged necessity for a new workhouse and have not been able to discover any documents or reports bearing upon the matter by their predecessors… They find that the workhouse proper contains ample for 800 persons and should there be pressure the branch establishments at Hollow Meadows can be made available for 300 more, making a total of accommodation for 1,100 persons. Your committee therefore report that there is no necessity whatever for a new workhouse, inasmuch as the present average number of inmates does not exceed 600 persons, and they further recommend the Board to decline all proceedings in reference thereto.

However, taking on the might of the Poor Law Board was more difficult than they had at first thought possible. The Guardians were forced to have most decisions about the running of the workhouse and appointment of staff sanctioned by the Board, who by now must have lost patience with the Sheffield Guardians. Meanwhile, the townspeople, in order to thank the Guardians for their stance against the Poor Law Board, held a meeting at the Town Hall on Monday, 19 October 1857. The chair of the meeting, Mr W. Harvey, congratulated the Guardians for not allowing 'the Poor Law Board to put their hands into our pockets', for which he was roundly cheered.

A year later the Guardians were still discussing what was to be done with the land which had been bought at Darnall. On Wednesday, 27 May 1857, the committee reported back to the Guardians that they were bound to complete the purchase of the land, which should have been completed the previous year. The land was costing them £140 a year in interest, and in their opinion 'there was no chance to escape from this dilemma'. The Guardians decided that they would send a deputation to the Poor Law Board to request an order rescinding the sale. The deputation pointed out that the piece of land was too far out of the town centre and that the Guardians would have to walk three or four miles to attend their weekly meetings. The deputation also stated that the enlargement of the present building on Kelham Street would provide all the necessary classification of the inmates to ensure that certain parties – such as the elderly, infirm, lunatics and imbeciles, and most importantly the 'itch and lock wards' – were kept separate from the other inmates. No decision was arrived at, but the Poor Law Board agreed to look at the plans for the enlargement.

At the next Board meeting the chair assured the other Guardians that, 'it seems that the Poor Law Board are determined to build a new workhouse and we are determined not to, and it is therefore necessary that we show a bold front'. An architect, Mr Cashin, drew up plans of the proposed enlargements, and they were sent with a report to the Poor Law Board. In short, the report stated that they:

> express an earnest hope that the Poor Law Board, now seeing the great capacity of the workhouse and the perfect way in which all their objections were met and remedied, will at once accede to the wishes of the Guardians and the ratepayers of Sheffield and thus put an end to the irritation and excitement that has so long existed and disturbed the peace of the union on the subject of the new workhouse.

But the Poor Law Board were not finished yet, and they refused to sanction the alterations, stating that 'a new workhouse was the only remedy for any existing evils'. On 9 June 1858, the Poor Law Board pointed out the overcrowding and ordered sixteen day and night wards to be closed. The Guardians complied by turning them into store rooms. They insisted that by enlarging the building such defects would be remedied, but the Poor Law Board 'refused to sanction any alterations to the present building'. On 27 November 1858 they sent a letter stating that the Inspector Mr Mainwaring had visited on 13 November and, accompanied by Mr Skinner, the Medical Officer, had found five more rooms were 'greatly overcrowded'. They were asked to reduce the numbers in those room and the Guardians replied that 'the overcrowding was the fault of the Poor Law Board themselves by closing down the other sixteen rooms previously.' They said that the situation would not have arisen if they had got sanction to make the proposed alterations and enlargements in the plan submitted to the Poor Law Board. The Guardians discussed what they should do and it was decided that they would have to put more of the inmates on outdoor relief and therefore reduce the numbers in the house. The chair agreed, stating that he would let the Poor Law Board make the next move but that if they insisted on closing any more of the rooms he would call a public meeting to ask the ratepayers: 'are you prepared to succumb to this central authority, or will you resist by granting more out-relief and thereby, no doubt, creating more pauperism'.

Realising that the situation was getting out of hand, the chairman of the Guardians approached a Sheffield MP, Mr Roebuck, to mediate in the difficulties with the Poor Law Board; he agreed to meet with the president of that Board, Mr Estcourt, on 12 March 1859 in Whitehall. The meeting was successful in that, at last, it seemed that the long-running and contentious issue of the building of a new workhouse was finally put to bed. On 25 May 1859 the plans for altering the workhouse were returned to the Sheffield Guardians with the affixed seal and approval of the Poor Law Board. The chair announced that 'finally the question of the alterations should now be considered as settled'. The Poor Law Board sanctioned a loan in September of 1859, and by 5 October the Guardians were finally given permission to sell the land at Darnall. They resolved to advertise the sale by auction, and the land was finally sold in November of 1859, when it raised the sum of £2,823.

By 22 December 1860 the enlargements were completed and the Guardians were satisfied that the new enlarged workhouse on Kelham Street could accommodate as many as 1,100 paupers. The chair spoke proudly, explaining that: 'the objections raised by the Poor Law Board to the retention of the present workhouse are now removed and adequate accommodation has been provided. There is now proper classification, better ventilation and good drainage secured and a vexed question settled for the next thirty years.'

Unfortunately, however, the question had not been settled – only fourteen years later, in May of 1874, Mr Basil Cane produced a report stating that, once again, Sheffield's workhouse was overcrowded. The visiting committee had agreed that a new workhouse was urgently needed in the town. He reported back to the Local Government Board, claiming that the majority of Guardians were in favour of a new house being built. In a further report, written by Mr Davy, the assistant Inspector, he added that the house was unhealthy and the drainage insufficient. One of the Guardians contested this on 31 September 1874, stating that 'the house was naturally adapted there being a fall of several feet into the river.' The master, Mr Ward, had supplied returns which showed that the house was healthy, and that the death rate for the paupers was superior to that of the town. Some of the population of Sheffield lived in very poor housing and street conditions. He further insisted that the numbers of paupers in the house had decreased rather than increased: from March 1858 to March 1859 the yearly number of paupers had been 7,097, but in the years 1873 to 1874 the number was 4,195. Mr Bacon disagreed. According to the report of Mr Cane, if the house was crowded during a period of relative trade prosperity then what would be the situation when adverse conditions returned? They would have to make provision for it. Somehow he managed to persuade the other Guardians that another, larger workhouse was needed, and a committee was asked to look at some suitable sites.

Two weeks later a piece of land measuring forty-two acres had been identified at a small farm situated at Fir Vale belonging to Thomas W. Cadman. It was reported that there was a stream of water running alongside the land, that water pipes had already been laid up to the building, and that access to it would be easy for the poor people of the town. Mr Cadman was willing to sell the land, with the timber thereon, for the sum of £13,500. The committee urged the Guardians to accept Mr Cadman's offer, and that an agreement be made with the sanction of the Local Government Board. By April 1874, Mr Basil Cane had seen the site and declared his approval. He told his colleagues that 'the situation was warm, there was an abundance of water and the land was everything they could have wished'. Later that month the Local Government Board sanctioned the borrowing of £60,000 to erect the building, and a further loan of £13,500 for the land at Fir Vale.

Thankfully, due to the great interest in workhouses towards the end of the nineteenth century, we have a very good external description of the Fir Vale workhouse. Mr R.J. Pye Smith, a professor at Sheffield University, described his visit to the workhouse, a trip which he undertook, with the permission of the chair of the Guardians, on 24 August 1896. He describes the entrance to the workhouse as having long avenues of poplar trees 'bright

A standard type of workhouse kitchen.

Dinner being served to ranks upon ranks of destitute paupers in a typical workhouse dining room.

Fir Vale hospital.

with nasturtium borders and well timbered woods beyond'. At the side of the garden was a field where 'a few men were at work wheeling earth' and he noted 'a crop of oats and large quantities of vegetables'. He described the house as 'a block of buildings close on a quarter of a mile long with isolated blocks springing up all over the estate'. The date on the foundation stone was September 1878, and he described the building as 'this great pauper palace'. (R.J. Pye Smith, reprinted from *The Sheffield Daily Telegraph*, 4 Sept 1896. Ref. No. AC67-3. Courtesy of Sheffield Archives)

A further description of the inside of the workhouse was given in the *Sheffield and Rotherham Independent* on 24 February 1881, which describes the main building. This part contained two wings, with the administrative part being in the middle, and many smaller rooms for the workhouse officials – as well as the Boardroom for the Guardians' meetings. A large stair ran from the entrance hall to the dining room (which would seat 700 persons, and was also used for religious services). The room was fitted with pitch-pine seats which were reversible and could also be used as tables. Beneath the dining room was the kitchen, which was described as 'gigantic in size where the food was cooked and delivered by lifts to the various wards'. Interestingly, it seems that a tramway was used in the basement corridors for the easy transportation of stores and other articles required in other parts of the house. The north wing, which was to the right of the kitchens, contained all the male wards for able-bodied, infirm and bedridden men. The lower rooms were devoted to day rooms 'where the male inmates can smoke, read or talk at their leisure'. The two upper storeys contained the sleeping rooms, the beds being arranged in a barrack fashion. At the back of this wing and across the courts used for airing clothes were the workshops, the oakum shed, joiners' shop, shoemakers' shop, a tailors' shop and a bake house.

The south wing was for the exclusive use of female paupers and was arranged in a similar fashion as the male side. The women's workshops at the back contained a laundry and sewing rooms. The schools were just beyond the north wing separated by a road 40ft wide. In the centre of the school building was a large dining hall which accommodated about 200 scholars. Near to the dining hall was a plunge bath and industrial shops for the boys consisting of tailors' shops and shoe shops, with sewing rooms and wash houses for the girls. To the east of the dining hall was the girls' and infants' school with accommodation for about another 200 children and to the west side was the boys' school. All the upper storeys contained the bedrooms, and the whole edifice was described as 'a colossal monument to the Poor Law system'.

The Fir Vale workhouse continued until March 1967, by which time the buildings contained two of the hospitals which were combined to make the Northern General Hospital, whose doors are still open today. Many people who enter the building are unaware that it started life as a workhouse.

four

Guardians of the Poor

The Poor Law Amendment Act empowered a Board of Guardians to be elected to deal with the day-to-day administration of the workhouse. However, Sheffield rebelled – pointing out that the Act could not be implemented if they refused to appoint Guardians. The Poor Law Assistant, Mr Gulson, was sent to speak to the ratepayers and overseers of the various Sheffield townships at the Tontine Inn on the Haymarket on Tuesday, 15 May 1837. He managed to reassure the people of Sheffield that hostility against the Act generally ceased once it was implemented, and that it was necessary that the appointed Guardians of the Poor should be elected. He pointed out that the Guardians would make the decisions about the amounts of relief to be awarded, stating that 'if they wished to double the relief paid to old people, for example, the Commissioners would have no wish to prevent it'. He praised the dietary table which the workhouse officers supplied, finding 'it was the most ample he had seen in many workhouses'. It was agreed that the Guardians would be appointed – but once again the ratepayer's opposition changed everything. Mr Gulson was sent back to Sheffield the following week, on 20 May 1837. He began by praising the way in which Sheffield had managed their parochial affairs, in particular the large numbers of paupers on out-relief. However, he pointed out the necessity for the appointment of a Board of Guardians before the deadline set by the Commission of 30 June 1837. Mr Gulson said that if he remained in charge of the district he 'hoped that they should continue on the same friendly terms as now'. Despite the friendly tone, the people of Sheffield and the authorities of other towns in the West Riding felt that much better co-operation should be found with a local government authority who better understood the issues affecting towns such as Sheffield. At the next ratepayers' meeting, a Mr Wigfall was sceptical of the praise heaped on the management of Sheffield by Mr Gulson: 'it appeared to him that Mr Gulson came amongst them very pleasantly… but that when he got the bridle on he would ride them as he pleased'.

A further meeting was held on Friday, 9 June 1837 at the Kelham Street workhouse, ostensibly to elect the Sheffield Guardians. The crowd that attended the meeting was almost 2,000 strong, and there was much opposition to both the election and the Act. Thomas Dunn was elected to the chair and when he told the assembled crowd that they

The Tontine Inn, Haymarket.

were here to elect the Guardians, there were cries of 'we won't have them' and the crowd erupted in an uproar. Mr Dunn explained that he knew of no way to evade the law but one: 'The Commissioners cannot compel them to nominate Guardians, but if they were elected the Commissioners could compel them to act or they might imprison them. He therefore knew of no way to evade this cruel and oppressive Act but to refuse to nominate the Guardians'.

Another ratepayer, Mr Luke Booth, also passionately stated his opposition to the Poor Law Commissioners, crying 'we should resist the introduction of that measure here or be slaves for ever!' Mr Wigfall pointed out that the most objectionable part of the Act was that the people of Sheffield would be subject to three Commissioners in London who had power to inflict arbitrary, unjust and cruel laws which, he was persuaded, the English would never submit to. Another ratepayer, Mr Lomas, declared, 'what a puppet piece of machinery the Poor Law was: at the one end of the string was the Chancellor of the Exchequer who moved the Commissioners, the Commissioners moved the Guardians and the Guardians moved the kingdom'. He continued in a similar vein: 'it involved their honour as men and as Englishmen and would carry down their names to posterity in such a way that their children need not be ashamed of their pedigree'. It was finally resolved that a committee be appointed to act in concert with the overseers and churchwardens to work against the implementation of the Act in Sheffield. The following week the overseers suspended the serving of the notices required to elect the Guardians. At a meeting of the Brightside ratepayers, on 19 June 1837, they recommended that 'the churchwarden and overseers do not carry the instructions of the Poor Law Commissioners into effect'. They also resolved to 'send a memo to His Majesty and the Privy Council to allow this township to remain under its present system'.

The *Sheffield Independent* supported the rebellion, and stated on 17 June 1837 that it had seen the regulations of the Commissioners, an overview into the control which the Commissioners would exercise through the overseers and the Guardians. Despite being assured that the Guardians would be able to fix the amount of relief, the regulations in fact stated that:

- No relief shall be given in money to any able-bodied pauper in employment.
- If any able-bodied pauper asks for relief one half of it should be given 'in kind' (usually bread).
- One half of relief given to widows or single women shall be 'in kind'.
- No relief shall be given to able-bodied paupers to cover rent.
- No relief shall be given to paupers not residing in their own parish.

A further meeting was called for 20 June and a resolution was forwarded to the Poor Law Commissioners to the effect that Sheffield would take no part in the election of the Guardians. According to the eighteenth clause of the Act, those who refused to carry out the orders of the Poor Law Commission would be fined between 40s and £5 each. It was stipulated further that those who refused to work to implement the Act, and demonstrated wilful disobedience to the Commission, would be fined £5 for a first offence, £20 for the second offence and receive a prison sentence for other offences. One of the ratepayers, a Mr Creswick, stipulated that 'he would have no share in the responsibility of bringing this obnoxious law into effect'. Despite the opposition, however, a reply was received from the Poor Law Commissioners which categorically stated:

> The Commissioner feels it right to state for your information and to prevent you unwittingly to commit an infraction of the law that their order under their seal dated 5th instant declaring the Sheffield Union and requiring the election of the Sheffield Guardians on the 30th June must in all respect be observed and that any parish officer omitting to carry out the orders and directions given shall subject himself to the penalties provided by the Act.

The letter stated clearly that after 30 June no amount of relief could 'be sanctioned and will therefore be considered illegal'. The overseers and the people of Sheffield were dismayed, and they knew that they had no option but to obey. The Sheffield Guardians would have to be elected. The election was carried out on the last legal day, 30 June.

The newly appointed Guardians agreed to meet every week on a Wednesday at the Boardroom at the Kelham Street workhouse, and despite their initial hostility they took on the task with relish. They appointed committees to further investigate issues which had arisen; these would report back to the Guardians on a weekly basis. A visiting committee rota was developed which required two Guardians to visit the workhouse every week: they were to inspect it and report any issues or complaints from the inmates. They also elected a clerk and other workhouse officials, all of whose positions had to be sanctioned by the Poor Law Commission. By 1847 the Poor Law authorities had issued the General Consolidated Order to aid the Guardians. This listed all the duties and responsibilities of every workhouse officer, and was seen as a 'Bible' for the smooth running of workhouses. The relationship between the Guardians and the Poor Law authorities had got off to a bad start, and the Sheffield Guardians continued to be very critical of the Commission. There are comments throughout the Guardians' meetings about what they saw as 'interference' with the decisions. By March 1860, various Boards of Guardians throughout the country were beginning to object to the sanctions which had to be sought from the Poor Law Board. The Guardians stated in their meeting that 'the Sheffield Guardians should be in

Reports of Brightside ratepayers' meeting, where Sheffield's residents refused to appoint new Guardians and resolved instead to force Her Majesty's Government to 'remain under its present system'.

a position to manage their own affairs'. On one occasion, when the auditor had disallowed some payments, the chair was heard to comment that 'the Poor Law auditors should just examine the books and not tell the Guardians how to spend the ratepayer's money'.

Almost from the first meeting, the Guardians' meetings were regularly being reported in the pages of the local newspapers – which characteristically listed all the jeering and catcalls which also took place during the meetings. The Guardians resolved in July of 1862 to make a decision as to whether reporters were to continue to cover the meetings in the local press. (This followed a pretty rebellious session the previous week which had been reported in full.) The chair pointed out that 'the scenes last week will make the public think that the Guardians don't do much work.' As if to negate this, he listed all the improvements in the workhouse which had been made during the previous year by the present Board of Guardians. He pointed out that the numbers of men on relief and the number of patients in the hospital had decreased in number. He stated that the stores were now kept excellently by Mr Westcoe, the master, and cryptically that 'all the male workhouse officers were doing their duty'. They came to no decision on that occasion about the reporters: the Guardians knew that if they banished them, the ratepayers of the town might wonder what the Guardians had to hide. The matter was brought up again later that month by Mr Crawshaw, who stated that there was no personal animosity in the matter, but felt that 'if the reporters were absent the Guardians would be much better friends'. Thankfully for future historians, no one seconded the proposal, which 'fell to the ground'.

Yet there were a few times of peace and harmony. During the last meeting before the elections were due to take place in March 1865, the chair, Mr Saunders, congratulated the other Guardians on the peaceful way that the meetings had been run, saying that: 'in previous years the meetings had been scenes of perpetual confusion, quarrelling and disagreements'. During the last year, however, 'there had been a kindly interchange of feeling and opinion'.

He talked about his work during the year as chair and the responsibilities which that task involved for himself and for the other members of the Board. He had to attend the workhouse on a Saturday to ensure that the meat and other supplies that had been delivered to the house were acceptable. He praised the work carried out by the other Guardians, reminding them that it was their responsibility to give relief to hundreds – if not thousands – of people. They also had the responsibility for the school at Pitsmoor, the lunatics at Wakefield and the farm at Hollow Meadows. He pointed out that each case which was brought before the Guardians had to be enquired into, which took up a lot of the Guardians' time. They had to make the decision of who deserved relief and who would become a burden on the rates. He also said that he felt that the ratepayers appreciated the amount of time and effort the Guardians spent on the work involved. However, this peaceful situation was not to last: after yet another confrontational meeting, one of the Guardians sent a letter to the clerk at the beginning of September 1868 giving his resignation. He wrote:

Cambria Works, Sheffield 31 August 1868

Dear Sir,

During the last few weeks I have been seriously considering my position as a member of the Sheffield Board of Guardians, and I am sorry to inform you that my sense of self respect has compelled me to announce my withdrawal from its deliberations. If I could have had any doubts about the propriety of this step they would have been entirely set aside by reading the report of the melancholy exhibition the Guardians made at their last meeting. I think the ratepayers will agree with me that it is a great misfortune that the affairs of such a large union should be entrusted to a Board whose great characteristics are vacillation and incompetence. I have no hesitation in saying that when the year is expired it will be found that the most egregious mistakes will be made and I decline to be responsible for or connected with such proceedings… You will oblige me by reading this letter to the Board on Wednesday next.

I am, dear Sir, yours faithfully,

Edward Dodson

One of the Guardians, Mr Jackson, sarcastically noted that none of them would feel his loss very much, 'for although he had been a Guardian for some time he hardly ever attended the meetings of the Board'. He suggested that his motivation sprung from resentment as 'he knew that he was a disappointed man'. It seems that when he was recently proposed as chairman of the Board no one had seconded his proposition. Another Guardian, Mr Searle, rebuked Mr Jackson for his unkindness: since 'it was Mr Jackson who proposed Mr Dodson, perhaps he was a disappointed man also'. The Guardians laughed and cheered at this before the chair intervened and called the Board to order. However, it was not long before the Guardians were criticized once again by one of their own. A letter was written by a previous chair, Alderman Saunders, and printed in the local newspaper (which was becoming openly critical of the workhouse Guardians). Despite the fact that Alderman Saunders had praised the Guardians under his chairmanship, in December 1868 he wrote:

I am sorry to admit that the ratepayers, officers and the poor all complain of the general neglect by the present Board in the performance of their duties and the whole working of the Poor Law is stagnated by general indifference, want of attention and knowledge on the part of the present Guardians.

One of the Guardians, Mr Jackson, referring to Alderman Saunders' letter, requested that his colleagues take no notice of the missive, claiming that 'he was doing it to get elected the following year'. It seems it was a good ploy, because Alderman Saunders was indeed elected to the chair in April 1869; even under his chairmanship, however, the insulting behaviour continued to be reported. There were further instances of upheaval when one of the Guardians, Mr Jackson, speaking in a later Board meeting, referred to Mr Hallam as 'a fraud' and 'a fool'; in June 1871 it was reported that 'after angry squabbles the business of the Guardians was concluded'.

There is no doubt that the people of Sheffield must have questioned the disreputable way in which the Guardians behaved while spending the ratepayer's money. So it was with some relish that in April 1879 a damning accusation was made: that the Guardians were going into the workhouse at late hours and eating and drinking with the master, Mr Ward, at the ratepayer's expense. There had been a rumour going around the town for quite a while that the Guardians were regularly 'partaking of fish, flesh and fowl and a good wash down (a drink) for 6d'. It was also alleged that some of them were leaving by the back gate instead of the front to prevent their names from being recorded by the porter. The matter was discussed with much levity in a Board meeting held on Wednesday 9 April. The chair pointed out that the stories implied that the Guardians were using the back door either because they were intoxicated, or because they were using the house for 'immoral purposes'.

One of the Guardians, Mr Hoyland, asked, 'Was it true that members of the present Board had been turned out of the pubs at closing time drunk and had been found in the early hours of the morning on the women's side of the house, but had left before the master came on duty?' This statement caused uproar in the Boardroom. The chair desperately attempted to quell the shouting. He vehemently denied the reports, claiming:

> A very respectable person came into the workhouse with the master between 9 p.m. and 10 p.m. He did not think that the complaints referred to him or any other member of the Board and that he was not afraid of Mr Hoyland or anyone else knowing what went on in the house.

The subject was then dropped, and the Guardians returned back to the business of the workhouse. The confrontations and accusations, however, continue to pepper the reports from the meetings. A complaint about the bad language which had been used at the previous Board meeting was reported in the press in June 1880. Once again, it was Mr Hoyland who brought the issue up, stating that terms like 'secret informers' and 'spies' had been made at this meeting. He pointed out that 'in the performance of their duties the Guardians needed to succour and support each other rather than indulge in such language'. Mr Hudson resented this accusation, and accused Mr Hoyland of being 'apt not to speak the truth'. Mr Hoyland leapt to his feet and demanded that he withdraw that statement as he had now said it on three separate occasions. He demanded that Mr Hudson 'withdraw it or prove it'. Mr Hudson finally withdrew the remark. But he spoke of the fact that there was a 'Judas Iscariot' on the Board who repeated all these arguments to the press. Certainly the Guardians' meetings were detailed in the local newspapers, and never more so than

The women's ward
at a workhouse in
around 1900.

IN A
WOMEN'S
WARD.

during the arguments for and against the question of the erection of a new workhouse in 1858. The press used headings such as 'squabbling about the erection of a new workhouse' and 'more squabbling over the erection of a new workhouse'. There was even one meeting where the Guardians argued about the actual number of paupers in the house.

Once the new workhouse at Fir Vale was opened, the Guardians held their meetings at the new offices on West Bar. The first meeting had been held there on Wednesday, 31 August 1881, and the clerk congratulated Alderman Searle as the first chair to the Sheffield Board of Guardians to hold the meetings in the new Boardroom. Mr Basil Cane, the Poor Law Inspector, was also in attendance, and he also added his congratulations, saying that he had visited the Boardroom at the old workhouse and it was 'very shabby indeed'.

An interesting discussion took place in West Bar Boardroom on Wednesday, 20 September 1899 while the Guardians were discussing the new Workman's Compensation Act, which had been introduced in July 1897. This new Act ensured that any workman injured at work would have to be recompensed by his employer. It appeared that Mrs Caroline Davy had recently been awarded £175 from Messrs John Brown and Co. after her husband had been killed at work. She had received part of the money, £65 (£10 being deducted for solicitor's fees), and the remainder had been put into the hands of a solicitor for the benefit of her five children. Mrs Davy had bought a pony and cart and set two of her older children up in the fruit trade. Since then, however, the pony and cart had been sold due to her heavy drinking, and she had gone into the workhouse. One of her children had been maintained in the workhouse with her and another child put into the one of the children's homes. The Guardians discussed whether they could reclaim any of

The new union offices on West Bar (nearest the camera).

the compensation for the maintenance of the family whilst in the workhouse. Mr Machin stated that the legal aspect of the affair had been signed and sealed. He proposed that if they now wanted to interfere and change it, that the mother might use this as a precedent to do the same. If she was successful, and spent the money, the family would be worse off than they already were, and it was agreed that they would leave the matter alone.

The following year the same Act was put to the test again. The superintendent of the Children's Home, Mr Offen, told that Guardians that a man named Quibell had fallen off a ladder whilst working at the home and had been injured. He had sent a doctor to see him, and was praised for his good attention to the man. The Guardians felt that Quibell would be unable to claim any compensation from them, as his ladder was less than 30ft high. It was agreed that his wages would be paid to him during the time he was off sick. The Guardians also discussed what would happen in the event that an accident happened to a pauper in the workhouse, but they agreed that, as paupers had no wages, the Act would not apply. All paupers who had jobs in the workhouse were always paid in extra rations rather than with money.

As we have seen, the Sheffield Guardians were not afraid to challenge each other during Boardroom meetings – but these arguments were as nothing to the tempest that broke out after a resolution in 1898 that the Board of Guardians should contain equal numbers of Conservative and of Liberals. All the various committees were also to have equal memberships, and as a result some members were forced to resign from those committees. One of the Guardians, Mr Thompson, pointed out that 'if the Conservatives wanted a trial of strength let it be clearly understood that the two parties on the Board were to be in open antagonism'. Other Guardians wanted to withdraw from some of the committees, whilst others had the decision made for them. Mr Wells Smith wanted to withdraw his name from the Estate and Works' Committee, stating that, 'the chairman says that he attended every meeting and I make a statement to the contrary. I cannot act with a chairman who says that'. The divisions appeared to make the Guardians more outspoken, if that were possible. At the next Boardroom meeting, Mr John Wilson loudly protested the 'nonsense' which had been discussed at the Children's Homes' committee, declaring that he was 'bored to death every Board day with these discussions'. Mr Hadfield tried to interrupt, but was told by Mr Wilson to sit down: 'you've said enough, you have been up seven times'. Just then the chair declared, 'order'.

The divisions and arguments continued to be reported widely, and yet it cannot be denied that the Guardians genuinely tried to do their best for the paupers of the town. This body of men were not afraid to take risks and to start new schemes – and nowhere was this more prominently displayed that in the development of two farming schemes to provide suitable work for the paupers of Sheffield.

five

Hollow Meadows and Doe Royd Farms

The Hollow Meadows farm was a leading experiment which was set up by the Sheffield Guardians to encourage able-bodied paupers to find some kind of dignity in the required work. The Guardians had taken note of the monotonous nature of the work provided by oakum-picking or stone-breaking (which was the same kind of work undertaken by convicts). It was felt that the inmates viewed this labour as a punishment which, if anything, broke men's spirits. By giving men work on a farm, the Guardians knew the inmates would find the work more productive and satisfying, and would be healthier as a result. Added to this was a bonus: the farm would provide a source of healthier provisions for the rest of the inmates.

In 1840, '41 and '42, there had been great depressions of trade in Sheffield, and the paupers claiming relief had been involved in such lowly tasks as road-making, breaking stones and sweeping the streets. The Guardians were forced to find any kind of work for the men to do and the combination of such degrading occupations and being out in all weathers had resulted in a mutiny of the paupers. The Hollow Meadow scheme had been actively promoted by one of the Guardians, Isaac Ironside, who was well known for his radical views on Chartism and rights for the working man. Not all the Guardians were in agreement, and some of them stated that it was a 'profitless expenditure of time'. Other types of test work had been tried and abandoned.

In May of 1848 the Guardians decided on a new and innovative kind of test work for the paupers, and the Hollow Meadows scheme began. The clerk of the Guardians, Mr John Watkinson, ascertained that a piece of land measuring fifty-two acres was available at the head of the Rivelin Valley. This was situated seven miles from the centre of Sheffield, on land which belonged to the Duke of Norfolk. Mr Isaac Ironside suggested that the paupers would now work on the farm, reclaiming scrubland which could be used to grow crops or rented out to local farmers. Initially a group of twenty-four men were set to work, and it was immediately noted that the men were more cheerful and healthier, with 'an increased capacity for labour and with a taste for country scenes and employment'. The Guardians were delighted with the early results of the experiment. By July 1848 a stone-laying ceremony was performed by Mr Wilson Overend Esq., who was Her Majesty's Inspector of the Peace. The Guardians decided to celebrate the event by inviting overseers, builders and principal ratepayers to the farm. It was reported in the local newspaper that:

> between 12 and 1 p.m. approximately 50 or 60 people started to arrive. A tent had been erected for the large dinner which was to be served. The stone itself was covered by an orange election flag with 'Free Trade and Cheap Bread' written on it. The Revd Harris gave a short prayer, 'God Save the Queen' was sung and dinner was served at 2.30 p.m. After 40 of the guests had eaten their dinner the remains were set on a table and servants, workmen and poor people helped themselves.

The chair of the Guardians spoke about the difficulty in providing decent work for the paupers. He said how the kinds of test work previously undertaken should not be the sort of occupations given to able-bodied men out of work through no fault of their own. He told the assembled crowd that men who have been employed on the Hollow Meadows farm for only seven weeks came 'as wretched looking and half-starved creatures [and] have now become strong, healthy and robust agriculturists'. The intention was that the men:

> will attend the farm at 1 p.m. on Monday and after eating their dinner will commence work until evening. They will stay at the farm until dinnertime on Saturday and after dinner they are free to go home to their families and seek work if need be. They will spend all Sunday with their families attending Sunday worship and return here on Monday. The men will take home 2s on Saturday and his wife will receive 4s and 1s for each child in his absence.

For once the Poor Law Commissioners and the Guardians were unified as supporters of the experiment: as they pointed out, even if the scheme failed the property could still be sold as a farm and buildings. The chair to the Guardians stated that Sheffield Guardians had led the way, and that 'he hoped that all able bodied poor would have occupations such as this'. Not wishing to waste a good opportunity, a plate was passed around the tent collecting 70s, which the chair stated 'would be given to the men before returning home on Saturday afternoon', a comment which was greeted with resounding cheers. The opening ceremony was deemed to be a great success and it was reported that the activities went on further into the evening. The farm buildings were to be built on a piece of land on lease for ninety-nine years at an agreed rent of £4 year. The site also had a further fifty acres of moorland, which they had on lease for twenty years at 4s a year. The plans for the buildings to be erected were displayed at the stone laying ceremony and showed the principle buildings would form a three-storey 'T' shape. As the reporter described it:

> the lower arm [has] a day room and two sleeping rooms over it overlooking a southerly aspect facing the turnpike road. The day room was to be 45ft by 18ft and 10ft high. Behind will be the washing rooms, closet and staircase etc. The upper stroke of the 'T' will hold the superintendent's house with three rooms 10ft square on each floor. The sleeping apartments will hold 30 beds and the whole of the attic storey will hold another 60 beds for the men.

The Hollow Meadows farm scheme was deemed to be so successful that a deputation from the Leeds Board of Guardians visited the farm on 11 November 1850 in order to report on the employment of able-bodied men in farm work. Accompanied by the superintendent, Mr White, they were shown the farm and all the buildings and the land. After examining the farm and talking to the paupers, they retired to the house where a question and answer session started. The accounts were presented to them, from which they noted that 519 men had been employed at the farm between 9 May 1848 and 30 September 1850. The largest number in any one week was fifty-eight. The chair of the Leeds Guardians asked the farm superintendent, Mr White, whether he could recommend this form of work for able-bodied paupers. He replied that he 'thought the Sheffield Guardians had acted wisely when they took the land and put the men to work. Within a very short period of time the health of the men sent to the farm had vastly improved'. The accounts of 1851 revealed that the costs of rent, seeds, manure and the superintendents' salary was only £166 for the year, whilst the produce had realized £228 – a profit of £62. The following year the costs were just £108, and the produce was £250, leaving a surplus of £142. At last the Guardians had found the type of scale work which would make a profit – and they were delighted.

All the men who worked at the farm had three good meals a day. The three types of paupers who would be occupied there were described in 1850: the first class involved aged and infirm paupers who lived permanently at the farm and worked eight hours a day; the second class of pauper were the less infirm men who remained at the farm working eight hours a day, but were allowed to go home on Saturday and return on Monday; the third class, which included able-bodied men, only worked for four hours a day, but had to walk from Sheffield and back every day (a total of fourteen miles). However, it was said that the majority of men preferred to walk from Sheffield every day rather than do the extra hours at the farm. Mr White proposed that over the winter months men employed on piece work at the farm should be provided with beds, which was agreed. It seems at this point that the experiment was bound for success, but problems were encountered caused by the cyclical nature of trade depressions in the town. The farm could only make a profit if there was a large amount of manpower involved. At times when industry was good, the number of able-bodied men would drop and the farm would become inefficient. Returns for the farm illustrated this: in January 1853, when there was only fifteen men employed at the farm, it inevitably became unprofitable. Another familiar issue, problems with a workhouse officer, also plagued the scheme, and it began to unravel.

The clerk to the Guardians, Mr John Watkinson, had been instructed in mid-August 1850 to prepare the financial reports for Hollow Meadows, so that they might be published in the local newspapers in November 1850. Mr Ironside wanted the people of Sheffield to enjoy the success of the scheme, but Mr Watkinson refused to comply with this request. The Guardians wrote to the Poor Law Commissioners asking them to compel the clerk to provide the reports, but they declined. They stated that, although it was not within the strict legal scope of his duties, the Commissioners could not see any reasonable grounds for him refusing to comply with the Guardian's wishes. Finally, Mr Watkinson agreed to 'voluntarily' supply the reports on 30 November, and presented them to the Guardians and the *Sheffield Independent*.

HOLLOW MEADOWS FARM IN ACCOUNT WITH THE
SHEFFIELD GUARDIANS OF THE POOR

30 September 1850 Debit	£ s d	£ s d
Preliminary Expenses,		£99 9s 9d
Stock account,		£417 13s 3d
Incidental expenses,		£70 9s 5d
Horse accounts,		£109 17s 3d
Manure and seed,		£307 2s 9d
Pig account,		£87 6s 8d
Superintendent's salary,		£131 15s 6d
Farm labourers' wages,		£144 6s 2d
Rent and leases,		£17 6s 0d
Building account,	£1010 1s 11d	
Fencing account,	£81 2s 9d	
Furniture and fixtures,	£234 4s 7d	£1311 9s 3d
Provisions account,	£661 0s 3d	
Relief,	£831 6s 10½d	
Clothing,	£73 8s 9d	
		£1571 15s 10½d
		£4298 11s 10½d

Balance brought down:
£715 9s 0d

	£ s d
By sundry credit to treasurer,	£113 0s 8d
Valuation of Mr F. Wood including improvements	
in ridding, draining, edge stones, gravel walks,	
evergreens, forest trees, privet, planting, tillage's	
tenant rights, farm produce, live stock, farm	
implements, masons, joiners tools and other	
miscellaneous articles	£572 10s 4d
Building, fencing, furniture and fixtures at cost	£1311 9s 3d
Provisions, relief and clothing	£1571 15s 10½d
Sundries in stock and accounts not included above	£14 6s 9d
Balance being loss	£715 9s 0d
	£4298 11s 10½d

EMPLOYMENT
FOR THE ABLE-BODIED POOR.

Our readers have been made aware from time to time of the measures recently adopted by the guardians of the Sheffield Union, after much enquiry and consideration, for the employment of the able-bodied poor chargeable to the union, in reclaiming a piece of waste land at Hollow Meadows. During the depression of trade in 1840, '41, and '42, when there were many able-bodied paupers, the principal employments were road making, breaking stones, and street sweeping. These employments involved almost all possible evils—the degradation of the men, the profitless expenditure of time and strength, cruel exposure to inclement seasons, and combined discontent, producing almost an insurrection. The guardians were so strongly impressed with a conviction that this system would not do, that in the new arrangements of the Workhouse they provided for the employment of the able-bodied at hand flour mills. By these the out-door exposure is avoided, but no other good is secured. The work is irksome, wasteful, and produces great dissatisfaction; and moreover, it cannot be extended sufficiently to employ a sufficient number of men at a time like this. Oakum picking has been made an auxiliary, but that is almost as bad as confinement without any employment at all. Driven from all these modes of employment by their unsatisfactory results, the guardians have at last commenced a great experiment. For many years past, cultivation has been gradually encroaching upon the moors in the neighbourhood of the town, and converting heaths into productive fields. The guardians have now undertaken to plant an establishment on the moors, capable of accommodating about 100 men, and finding there their able-bodied poor to be employed in reclaiming waste land. We shall not here recapitulate the arrangements, which our readers will find well stated in the speech of Wilson Overend, Esq., the chairman of the board. We commend it to the careful consideration of the rate-payers. About two months ago, some 20 or 24 men began operations on the land, which is just beyond the Surrey inn, at Hollow Meadows, on the right-hand side of the turnpike road, in getting stone and preparing the site for the new buildings. We saw some of the men at that time. We saw some of them again on Monday, and we can fully corroborate the remarks of Mr. Overend as to their improved appearance and cheerfulness. Whenever trade calls them back to the town, they will come with a higher sense of their own value as men, with confirmed health, with increased capacity for labour, and with a taste for country scenes and employments which we trust will never leave them.

Report on the work for men at Hollow Meadows farm.

Mr Watkinson stated that 'it seemed to him that the Guardians had wanted to make him a kind of messenger to the newspapers, and he hoped that the Guardians would now see that there was some limit to their power'. He said that whilst waiting for the report to be prepared, the Guardians had been openly critical about him in the Boardroom meetings, which had been publicised, claiming that 'the conduct of the clerk was reprehensible and detrimental to the public service'. He had felt slighted by: 'The course which you thought proper to take, you certainly began and have continued in a way which has led to results very unfavourable to my reputation. In this manner reports have gone abroad and by some are believed and this places me in a light no better than that of the worst delinquent.'

Against the wishes of the majority of the Guardians, the actions of the clerk were defended by Mr Ironside, whose prime motivation was to see the experiment at Hollow Meadows a success. This naturally caused some antagonism between the Guardians and their clerk. It was claimed in February 1851 that Mr Watkinson had occupied much of his time with the running and 'mismanagement of Hollow Meadows farm'. A committee of seven of the Guardians was asked to complete a report on the working of the farm, which was presented by them at the Board meeting on 14 February 1851. The report condemned 'the confused, careless and irregular manner in which the financial accounts of the farm had been kept'. The report continued:

> Although the experimental nature of the work has been a great success and the attitude of the men to the work of clearing land for farming was conducive to their health, the management of the farm had been left to the clerk and as a result had cost the ratepayers dear. His inexperience, want of knowledge and lack of farming experience along with great extravagance have occasioned a large and unnecessary outlay.

It had not only been a cost to the ratepayers, but it was also noted that Mr Watkinson had kept at Hollow Meadows the parish horse and phaeton for his own convenience. The report continued that he had been required to place all accounts and letters before the Guardians at their weekly meetings, but this he refused to do. The Guardians wanted to be rid of John Watkinson. After all the bad publicity caused by his actions, it was hoped that the farm would prove successful. But only a year later the farm was being criticised once again for the high costs to the ratepayers. The main reason for this was supposed to be the inexperience of the men involved in the farming. One of the Guardians, an ex-farmer himself, stated in February 1851 that every load of wheat that had been grown on the farm, which was worth 15s, had cost the Guardians 30s. It was agreed that, instead of growing crops at the farm, the test labour for the paupers would be confined to clearing the land. Once the fifty acres of land had been cleared then, it was hoped, small plots of land would be let out to more experienced farmers.

The complaints against Mr Watkinson ceased for a while, until, on 16 November 1853, he finally overstepped the mark. It was unanimously resolved that he had 'set the Board at defiance' by: 'having carelessly lost or disingenuously kept back a letter from the Chesterfield Union requesting this union to relieve one of their aged paupers thus involving grievous wrong by delay. Also by addressing language calculated to give great pain and distress.' The chairman was requested to write to the Poor Law Commission to enquire whether this conduct on the part of the clerk had their sanction. The books were sealed in the meantime. Interestingly, one of the Sheffield workhouse letter books has had several pages torn out (between pages 693–698 and also 707–720, pages which date between 1847 and 1851). Was this the work of Mr Watkinson trying to hide some evidence of his mismanagement? We shall never know. But, as always, matters did not go easily for the Sheffield Guardians, and an enquiry, held by Mr Farnall, started on 28 December 1853. The Commissioners agreed that they could not consent to keeping him in his office, and they asked for his resignation. However, he demanded that a further enquiry be made, as he felt that his defence had not been heard. A further enquiry was held on 9 and 10 February 1854. Watkinson was defended by Mr Wilson Overend, and on 1 March they ordered him to resign. However, in true Sheffield form, he refused.

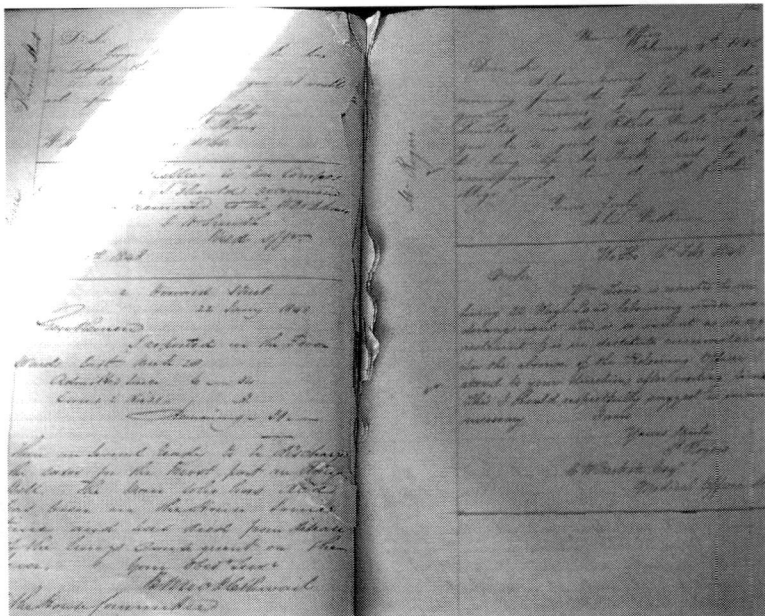

Torn out sheets from the letter book. Was this the work of the clerk, Mr Watkinson?

THE HOLLOW MEADOWS FARM.—A letter to the Union Clerk from Mr. Mainwaring, Poor Law Inspector, referring to his visit to the Hollow Meadows Farm on the 21st instant was read. It was dated Doncaster, 24th of August and requested the clerk to bring the matter at once under the notice of the guardians. It contained the following:—

"From what I observed and heard from the master, Mr. White, the existing arrangements for testing the destitution of able-bodied men must be a complete failure; and if the place is to be longer used, it is very desirable that it should be frequently visited by a committee of guardians, to be appointed for the purpose, that their reports may be brought before the board of guardians from time to time, and they be made acquainted thereby with its actual state, and the probable use it may be of for the object for which it is intended; and moreover, their periodical visits would have the effect of proper order and decorum being observed, which I regret to say, appear to be very little attended to.

"About 150 persons were at dinner when I reached the place, some of whom, for want of room in the dining room, were getting their dinners at the door, and in other parts of the premises; and one man was eating his dinner under the wall on the opposite side of the high-road, and was giving a portion of it to his boy, who was there ready to partake of it.

"Most of those sitting at dinner in the dining-hall had their hats or caps on, without observing the common habits of decency at meals.

Report of paupers sharing food with families at Hollow Meadows farm.

The Guardians resolved to hand his notice in for him in two weeks' time, and on 22 March Mr Joseph Spencer was elected in his place.

Finally, by 27 May 1857, the Guardians admitted that the experiment at Hollow Meadows farm had failed, and that it had cost them in the region of £100 in losses each year. At that time there were only five paupers at the farm, and on one occasion it was reported that there had been only one. The main argument against the farm was that it was seven miles out of the centre of Sheffield, and that many men had complained about working for five or six hours a day after walking for fourteen miles (total). The Guardians had initially seen this as a bonus, as one of them had stated that 'you won't find an idle vagabond walk up there and do the allotted work and then walk back'. Other Guardians disagreed, and one in particular, named Dr Flory, called the walk to the farm an 'exceedingly cruel act of tyranny on the part of the Guardians'. Discussions were made as to whether or not they should provide transport for the able-bodied men, but the idea was abandoned as being unprofitable.

In August of 1858 a report had been sent to the Guardians following a visit by Mr Mainwaring, the Poor Law Inspector, on the 21st of that month. He had held discussions with the farm Superintendent, Mr White, and requested that, if the farm was to continue, a visiting committee attend the farm regularly, 'which would have the effect of proper order and decorum being observed which is lacking at the moment'. He complained about the fact that all the men working at the farm received three substantial meals a day. He himself had observed the following scene:

There were about 150 paupers being served their dinners, some men who were unable to sit down in the dining room were eating it stood up against a wall. Another was eating his dinner leaning against a wall on the high road and giving a portion of it to his son. Many of these men were eating their dinner with their hats or caps on without observing the common habit of decency at meals. A man named James Mitchell with two daughters was sharing food with them and another man was taking his portion of bread which was well buttered and a piece of meat inside to take home for the following day (Sunday). Another man named John Mason, who was 19 years of age, was there earning the equivalent of 5s a week at a time when harvest work was plentiful. Why wasn't he seeking work instead of costing the ratepayers £1 a month?

This was an issue he had raised with the Guardians before; his past complaints included the fact that the Sheffield Guardians paid out more relief than other neighbouring towns.

He pointed out that many of the inmates of Sheffield workhouse were reluctant to find work outside of it. On the day of the inspection he had questioned a father who worked on the farm, a man with a wife and seven children. He had admitted to earning 9s a week; his eldest child, aged twelve, was able to earn 2s or 3s a week. When Mr Mainwaring asked him why he could not get a job in the town, he was frankly told that it was not worth his while. Mr Mainwaring also complained that the men who resided at the farm were in the habit of going out when and where they chose after 6 p.m. Many went to gather the bilberries which grew in abundance in the area, which they sold for 6d a quart. He strongly recommended that the paupers not be allowed outside the house after completing their work. The Inspector was so incensed at what he saw that he strongly recommended that the Guardians expel all the paupers from the farm and put them to work at the workhouse picking oakum or breaking stones. He asked Mr White for a list of the men who had been the longest at the farm and the list confirmed his opinion, and threw 'considerable doubt on the efficacy of the farm'.

The Guardians were quick to answer the comments made by Mr Mainwaring. At a Board meeting in November 1858 they replied to his criticism that the men had three meals in the six hours they were at work: fresh air and strong exercise entitled them to the full amount of sustenance allowed. As to children eating with their parents, Master White reminded the farm staff of Article 10 of the General Consolidated Order, that all paupers should take their meals in the dining room and no other place whatsoever. He also instructed that no pauper be allowed to carry away any food from the dining room. As regards the bilberry collecting, the Guardians pointed out that the owners of the moors had thrown them open for only two days. As the bilberry season lasted only for a few weeks, it had not been taken seriously by the Guardians. The difficulties experienced were partly due to the enormous amounts of men on relief at that time. They pointed out that in the months of February and March, 'there were upwards of 1,000 men claiming relief, of which 300 were employed at the farm.'

There then followed one of those rowdy scenes which often occurred in the Sheffield Guardians' meetings. One of the Guardians took exception to the farm Superintendent Mr White, for informing Mr Mainwaring of 'matters that he ought to have first communicated with the Guardians themselves'. But the chair defended him, saying that Mr White was a 'poor, simple and ignorant man and gave information unwittingly to one who was quite accustomed to such inspections'. Dr Flory suggested that the Poor Law Board were 'constantly carping at [the Guardians'] actions in order to bring about their grand scheme for a new workhouse and that the Poor Law Board did all they could to annoy them'. Once again it seems the Guardians had forgotten that such statements would be reported in the local newspapers. Not surprisingly, the following week a sharp letter was received from Mr White, hotly declaring that:

> your chairman has taken an unwarranted liberty with my character as published in the *Sheffield Independent* newspaper for last Saturday… and that whatever he will say in the disparagement of me will not lessen me in the estimation of rate payers who can and do appreciate my services to the union. I have had the care and responsibility of controlling of between 200 and 300 men at this isolated place, seven miles from headquarters, and not

one case went before the magistrates. But for the chair to call me 'a poor, simple ignorant man' is unfair, exceedingly impolitic, ungentlemanly and very discouraging. My wife, my daughter and myself have worked very hard from morning till bedtime very frequently as may be imagined in having to provide three meals a day for such a great number of men.

The chair explained that he believed Mr White to be a good officer; the comment was made to exonerate him of having made certain statements without first communicating them to the Guardians. Peace was finally restored.

The experiment of the farm had not been an unmitigated success as was at first hoped. The scheme had foundered under the sheer numbers of men who needed it during times of industrial depression set against the sharp decrease of numbers felt at other times. The costs of the farm were just too high, and so it was with some relief that the chairman reported at a Board meeting in August of 1858 that he had received a deputation from the Sheffield Reformatory School committee offering to take the farm off the Guardians' hands. It was resolved that a committee should be formed to assess the situation and to confer with the Reform School committee. During the meeting, adverse comments were of course reported. One of the Guardians, a Mr Mitchell, stated that, 'I should like to get rid of that nasty farm'. Another Guardian, Mr Eccleston, who had supported the experiment, said he felt that the farm 'was the best place for able-bodied men' and that it was 'better than placing them among a lot of idle fellows here in the Kelham Street workhouse'. It was eventually decided that the experiment should continue and a farm committee was developed in order to bring any issues to the Guardians' attention at their weekly Board meeting. This seems to have improved matters somewhat, and the working of the farm continued.

At a Board meeting held on 23 August 1861 one of the Guardians, Mr Watkins, requested that the paupers at Hollow Meadows be given a day's holiday on Monday 28 August. The day was to be one of celebration, and included an invitation to the Guardians of the 1848 committee, who had been instrumental in setting up the experiment, to go back to the farm and see all the improvements that had been made. A report of the visit was published in the *Sheffield and Rotherham* Independent on 31 August. Mr Watkins spoke of his sadness at the present industrial distress in the town and how it grieved him to see hundreds of able-bodied men walking to the farm and back home again. He could not offer any alternative at that time. Many men were out of work and the conditions in the town were very bad. Slums were prevalent, and it was thought that working on the farm would provide a healthier environment for the men. However, for the time being it was agreed that in some ways Hollow Meadows was a great success, as they had by then cleared 252 acres of land. The Guardians toasted its continuance.

Observations made by the farm committee on 13 November 1861 suggested that supervision was growing lax. Mr Mainwaring attended the Board meeting to discuss the work given to the men employed at Hollow Meadows. It was agreed that the men would have to provide evidence of their working day and attendance sheets would have to be signed by the work superintendent. The experimental nature of the farm seems to have been forgotten when it was stated that the Guardians had sent the most irredeemable paupers there on 10 November 1861. When Mr Mainwaring asked the reason, he was told

Mr Philip Ashberry.

that 'these were the most incorrigible paupers who it was thought that a bit of farm work would not do them any harm'. When he once more suggested that the men be employed at the Kelham Street picking oakum, he was told that the men would rather walk fourteen miles a day and work on the farm rather than work in the house.

Hollow Meadows was in the end a failure. Costs were high and the inexperience of the men and the superintendent ensured the farm was not a viable option. Despite the well-meaning intention of providing a healthier employment for men of the workhouse, the farm could not be supported as a loss. But the main reason for the failure was once again political: it was used by its instigator, Mr Isaac Ironside, to crush Philip Ashberry, who had been very critical of Mr Watkinson. Ironside supported and defended John Watkinson in all his endeavours (even when it was obvious that the man was incompetent). Eventually the farm was handed over to the newly created Sheffield School Board for use as an Industrial School for Truants in March 1879, and later it became the site of Hollow Meadows hospital.

The Sheffield Guardians remembered their high hopes for the farm and the better test work it had provided, and once again the idea of having a farm was heard in the Boardroom in March 1896. An extraordinary meeting was held where it was proposed to take on another farm, called Doe Royd, which consisted of a farmhouse and outbuildings and 160 acres of land; the lease was to commence on 1 May. The property, which had a yearly tenancy of £224, included four cottages and the stock (which was proposed to be taken on as a going concern). The Guardians, after learning their lesson at Hollow Meadows, proposed that a man and wife be appointed as an experienced farm bailiff and dairymaid. It was agreed that the farm bailiff would have to be a competent farmer and be able to keep books. He would also employ experienced farm labourers. The scheme must have been popular, as a few weeks later it was reported that fifty-four applications had been received by the newly created Farm Committee. It was agreed that Mr Dunstan and his wife would be appointed as Farm Bailiff and Dairy and Poultry Keeper at a joint salary of £78 p.a. The couple would have to give a surety of £200 for 'the faithful discharge of

Pigs sold by Hollow Meadows Farm Committee, 1891.

their duty'. Surprisingly, less than a year later, in April of 1897, the Dunstan's resigned and another couple were appointed in their place. It was initially agreed that the farm could be used to employ some of the children and that boys from the children's homes would be sent to the farm to pick stones from the fields and weed turnips. However, three months later this part of the scheme was abandoned when it was noted that the children were mingling with adult paupers. It was agreed that in future 'no children were to be sent to Doe Royd farm unless they can be safeguarded from such contact'.

The first meeting of the farm committee on 5 May 1896 agreed that the farm hands and paupers would have two extra meals during the harvest time, when they would have to work late, and that they would be entitled to 6d a day in lieu of beer. A labour master, Mr Quibell, was offered his existing wages and one of the cottages to live in at the farm to supervise the labour. The other three cottages were to be made ready for the twelve paupers who would work and live at the farm. It seems that, at last, the farm was a going concern, as it was decided that in September of the same year the number of cows would be fifty and the same number of cows should be maintained in the future. By November it had been decided that to supply sufficient milk to the workhouse and the children's homes a new dairy was needed, and that 'a present shed used for coal and a closet would be pulled down and a new dairy erected in its place'.

However, the Guardians were less lucky in April 1897, when a pig bought from a neighbouring farm developed swine fever and the whole lot of the pigs, valued at over £50, had to be destroyed. Nevertheless, the Guardians were delighted to report that the first year the farm had made £3,038 10s 10d profit. Cows and pigs were now regularly bought and sold at the farm.

The chair stated that he was delighted with the Doe Royd farm. The weekly accounts showed that there had been a profit of over £200, as well as a supply of much-improved provisions to the workhouse. Nevertheless, he pointed out that the reason for the farm was not to make a profit, but to improve the condition of the men working there. The farm continued to flourish until the end of this period of study. It seems that the Sheffield Guardians had learned their lesson by the failure of Hollow Meadows, and a greater watch was kept on the farm and the men employed there.

six

Pitsmoor Schools

The Sheffield Guardians and the Poor Law authorities were deeply concerned about the lives of children in the workhouse. It was accepted that children were there through no fault of their own and could only be corrupted by the experience. Many people genuinely believed that workhouse children were degraded by their own parents, who had already proved to be idle and shiftless by having to go into the workhouse. Generally speaking, the Victorians only saw what they wanted to see, and they didn't like to acknowledge that in the town itself many poor children were living on the streets. On Wednesday, 2 March 1881 the condition of street children was brought to the attention of the editor of the *Sheffield Independent* by Mr A.G. Tweedie. He wrote about the numbers of these children that had no homes and were begging for a living. Some town philanthropists had started to feed them, and as a consequence he stated that 'they are increasing in number'. He asked that a Boys' Refuge be established for them. He told the editor that a similar scheme had been started in Manchester, where such children were given a uniform to wear and encouraged to sell newspapers. I have been unable to find evidence of whether such a scheme was established in Sheffield, but the newspaper reported the following month that over 1,000 of these poor children had been given a treat at the Sheffield Temperance Hall 'where they received a substantial meal and were given a magic lantern show accompanied by a piano'.

One of these street children was brought into the Kelham Street workhouse in November 1847. She was called Jane Toothill, aged eleven, and she had been brought before the Bench for begging on the streets. She had been found in the neighbourhood of Water Lane and had told the police officers that she had been sent out to beg by her father, who 'was nowhere to be found'. The Mayor ordered her to be sent to the workhouse until some news was heard about her parents as she now had no home and was therefore destitute.

Because of the urgent need to remove children from adult paupers, as early as 13 April 1804 a public meeting was held in the Cutlers Hall to discuss the need for a separate workhouse for children. There is no evidence of whether this separate building was built for children at this time in Sheffield. In March 1843 the Poor Law Commissioners

Sheffield Cutlers Hall, where the meeting was held on 13 April 1804.

recommended that the old Pitsmoor workhouse, which had been built in May 1801, could be turned into an Industrial School for children and a meeting of the Pitsmoor ratepayers was held. They could not reach agreement, however, and the subject was left in abeyance. Two months later, on 18 May 1843, a further meeting was held by the Pitsmoor ratepayers in the workhouse yard. Mr George Wall, the senior overseer, stated to the assembled people that the meeting had been called to ascertain what the views of the ratepayers of Pitsmoor were in this matter. The people of Sheffield and Pitsmoor were only too aware of the plight of abandoned children. Mr Wall stated that 'at the present time there were too many outcast children driven to begging in the streets as was done by too many to the disgrace of the town'. Often children were abandoned by their parents in the street and it was the duty of the police to send them into the workhouse. The following note, dated 27 September 1847, requested the master to take in such children from an unsigned police constable. He wrote: 'Sir, I am directed by Mr Raynor to inform you that the two children Hugh Carol and Mary Carol are taken out of the street and wishes you to receive them and he will have the mother apprehended.'

Nevertheless, the Pitsmoor ratepayers were not willing to use the workhouse as a school for children. Mr Wall informed them that if they did not agree the Guardians would build an Industrial School elsewhere and the ratepayers of Pitsmoor would be forced to contribute towards the cost. He stated that: 'at this moment there were some children in this union and some in Sheffield workhouse living in every room from the bottom to the top without order or regularity. There could be no doubt that the children would be greatly benefited by being brought here, their comfort being increased and their health promoted'.

It was also agreed that if the workhouse was turned into an Industrial School the girls would be taught to wash, clean and iron clothes and learn all the domestic routines of a large establishment. The boys would be trained to mend shoes, sew clothes and 'to give them the habits of industry which would make them valuable apprentices to any trade'. He pointed out that he had seen the plans for the Industrial School at Pitsmoor, which had already been approved by the Commissioners, and the cost of altering the present building would be £6,000. However, he warned them that if a new Industrial School was to be erected elsewhere it would cost the ratepayers £20,000. At this comment there was uproar from the assembled crowd. The ratepayers agreed that the Pitsmoor workhouse would be used as schools for the children of Sheffield. At the Board meeting held at Kelham Street in June 1843 the Guardians were informed of the decision of the Pitsmoor ratepayers and noted that 'there were 300 children in the workhouse at present, and most of them were orphans or children of lunatics or persons otherwise disabled from providing for them'. The sanction of the Poor Law Commissioners was gained, and six months later all the children over five years of age were removed from the Kelham Street workhouse and established in the Pitsmoor Schools.

There were four different schools established for older boys and girls and infant boys and girls of between two and five years of age. The Guardians and the Poor Law authorities were delighted that the children were away from the disturbing influence of older paupers. Due to the lack of kitchens at Pitsmoor, the children returned to the Kelham Street workhouse for meals; to get there they were marched through the streets accompanied by the schoolmaster and schoolmistress.

At this time there were no formal educational requirements for workhouse teachers, who were expected to be on duty from early in the morning to last thing at night. An outline of the duties of the schoolmaster and schoolmistress was recorded in the letter book in July of 1848. It was put in the form of questions to be answered by the teachers, and it does cast doubt on the education of the two teachers answering the questions: the word 'scholastic', for example, is written as 'schoolastic'. The questions and answers were as follows:

Q. What are there [sic] duties in the morning prior to the opening of the school?

A. To superintend and instruct the children in all the habits of life. How to rise, dress and cleanse and to conduct themselves with order and decency in their dormitories. To inspect their person and their dress previous to their appearing in the hall for worship and meals and to conduct themselves orderly there. To superintend them whilst there and see that they are properly supplied and ensure that no breach of discipline takes place amongst them. To present to the master's office the Diary of Proceedings every morning at 8 a.m.

Q. Do they assist the master and matron in the dining hall and if so how?

A. Assist in superintending and distribution of the meals to them. Teaching children the observance of order and ceremony necessary and in conducting them orderly out of the hall.

Q. What time does school start and finish in a morning?

A. School is open for schoolastic [sic] teaching at 9 a.m. and finishes at 11.40 a.m.

Q. What time does school open in the forenoon?

A. Schoolastic teaching 2–5 p.m. except when the children are taken out of the town for air.

Q. What are the duties outside of school?

A. Everything appertaining to the training of the children is superintended by the schoolmaster. Their schoolastic instruction and industrial pursuits, clothing, time at meals, recreation: private, domestic and social and habits. At all times guarded and assisted by master and matron as needed but only by actual interference when teachers are away on leave.

Q. Does the schoolmaster have any help?

A. An elderly female pauper attends to the boys at night.

Q. What are the average weekly numbers of children in the school?

A. Boys from 43–60 and girls 30–40.

Q. Do both teachers reside in the workhouse?

A. Yes.

It seems by the questions and answers that the teachers had equal duties and responsibilities of caring for the children with the master and matron. Permission to leave the workhouse for any reason had to be granted by the workhouse master. No doubt this made the teachers feel that they were as much inmates as the paupers themselves. Relationships between the schoolteachers and the master were often fraught, and the subject of frequent complaints to the Poor Law authorities: the disparity between a master who was largely uneducated and the school master and mistress who felt that they should not be answerable to such a person was usually the root of these complaints. In March 1857 the schoolmaster, Mr Heeley, sent a letter to the visiting committee complaining about having to get permission from the master, Mr Rogers, to leave: 'he does not think that you believe that he should be imprisoned at Pitsmoor'. He requested that he be allowed to go out of the school twice a week, on Monday and Saturday evenings from 7.30 p.m. to 9 p.m., and once a month on Sunday, from 6 p.m. to 9 p.m. Not an unreasonable request – but there is no recorded answer to his plea.

Matters were made worse because the teachers believed that the master, Mr Rogers, had no jurisdiction over the school. The Pitsmoor School was roundly criticized by the chair of the Guardians, Mr John Merrill, in May 1857. He complained of the unsatisfactory education of the workhouse children, and stated that most of the children under ten years

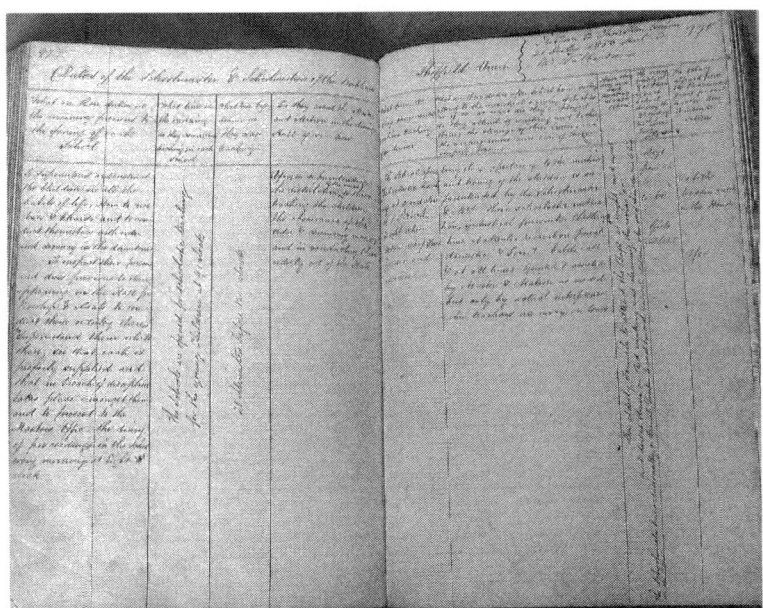

Duties of the
Sheffield Workhouse
schoolteachers.

of age were unable to read. It was, he insisted, 'the worst managed school in England'. In a report which appeared in the local newspaper, Mr Merrill attributed the lack of the children's literacy to the incompetence of the teachers. At a meeting the following week a letter was read from the schoolmaster, Mr Heeley, refuting this statement and saying that two other Guardians had visited the school and had been very impressed with the pupils. The two Guardians were Mr Hurst and Mr Eccleston. Both admitted to having visited the school following Mr Merrill's critique the previous week. They asked the schoolmaster to get the boys to stand up and read part of the fourteenth and fifteenth chapter of St Luke, and had to admit that the reading was poor. They then went to the girls' section – where they were quite surprised to find that fourteen or fifteen girls stood up to read. One girl, of only seven years of age, was described as 'a very proficient reader', and the two Guardians left the school suitably impressed. Mr Merrill retracted his statement at the next Board meeting, saying that perhaps it was just the boys' side which needed improvement.

There are two entries in the letters book which indicate the ignorance of another (unnamed) teacher at the school. The entries were written in 1847. One is a copy of an envelope badly addressed to the schoolmistress and covered with spelling mistakes. A disgusted notation has been appended to the side of it declaring that the envelope had been addressed by the 'teacher's son'. A further reference, written by a teacher who signed herself 'S. Barker', was also included in the letter book. It read: 'Isabelle Marr is the best girl I have in school, a very neat seamstress and an obedient child in her own conduct. She can repeat many hymns by art.'

There are several letters written by Mr Rogers to Mr Heeley containing severe warnings to him about punishing the children. They indicate that the relationship between the master and Mr Heeley was not good. The master sent him a letter, dated 5 June 1857, outlining the regulations regarding punishment 'which he may deem necessary to inflict on the children'. He reminded him that he was 'not allowed to deprive any child of the usual meal'. Mr Heeley retorted on 20 April 1857 that when he tried to inflict the slightest punishment on the children he had the words 'I will tell the master flung in his teeth'. He informed the master that he was aware that he had instructed the children to tell him when any punishments were made. The relationship between the teacher and his pupils continued to deteriorate, and this probably impacted on the discipline of the children. He informed the Guardians in July 1857 that: 'at dinner time today the following boys absconded and have not yet returned: Isaac Blaymires, John Scholey, John Goodwin, William Donald, Thomas Houson, William Stadfield, Daniel Sullivan, William Harvey and William Doud.'

He was reminded that the names needed to be entered in the schoolmaster's punishment book, which would then be presented to the Guardians. By now discipline must have completely broken down, as later that month thirteen more boys absconded, each of whom he claimed 'had not sufficiently been deterred by punishment'. Matters continued to worsen, and it was with some relief, no doubt, that he handed in his notice. He was replaced by Mr Robert Charlesworth on 9 December 1857. Only six months later Mr Charlesworth was complaining that Mr Rogers was refusing him leave of absence from the workhouse, and accusing the master of 'uncourteous conduct'. The master denied this to the Guardians, though he added that: 'I do admit that from the time of his appointment I believe it to have been an unfortunate one and I have studiously avoided any intercourse or interference with him'.

No doubt due to this poor relationship it was agreed by the Guardians that a committee must be appointed to look deeper into the workings of the school. One of the first difficulties revealed was that the order at the school was not well kept, as the school had been mainly run by the schoolteachers themselves. As a result of this it was proposed in June 1858 that the management of the school be taken over by the Guardians. The school teachers were to report to them every week in writing on the conduct of the children. They could also report any requirements of books, clothing or any other items necessary for the smooth running of the school. It was agreed that if the schoolteachers wanted leave of absence it would be sanctioned by the Guardians, and that leave 'must not in any way interfere with the proper discharge of their duties'. The same month Mr Charlesworth made a complaint to the local newspapers that the master had not let him know that the School Inspector was arriving. The master claimed that this was false, as was the schoolmaster's further statement that he had only been absent from the school on four occasions in six months: the master had checked the porter's book and found that the schoolmaster had in fact been absent thirty-nine times. The following month, on 3 July 1858, the Guardians received the resignation of the schoolmaster. It was agreed at the next Board meeting that an advertisement be inserted in the local newspapers for a schoolmaster. The Guardians requested a man that was 'competent in singing' as this 'would improve the children's moral character by furnishing them with a means to enjoy innocent recreation'. Only one of the Guardians opposed the resolution, stating it to be the 'thin edge of the wedge and we should soon want a piano for the workhouse next'.

Letter from Mr Heeley to Mr Rogers where the slightest punishment on the children has the words, 'I will tell the master flung in his teeth'.

Letter from Mr Rogers defending himself about the reports which Mr Charlesworth made to the press regarding the School Inspector's visit.

Letter from Mr Charlesworth accusing the master of 'uncourteous conduct'.

The school was now regularly inspected by the visiting committee, and further problems were brought to light in January 1859. The chair of the Guardians reported that he had found a lady visitor sitting in a school room with twelve boys, to whom she was teaching arithmetic. Other boys in the same room were endeavouring to write, and subsequently there was much confusion and noise. The schoolmaster had told the committee that there were several women visitors who constantly interrupted his classes. Whilst applauding the fact that these philanthropic women gave up their time to visit the workhouse children, it was resolved that the clerk should inform the schoolmaster that 'it is the wish of the Guardians that he must not allow any visitors without the sanction of the Board of Guardians'. Before long the Guardians were embroiled in yet another publicised disagreement in the press. A letter was sent protesting this ban to the editor of the *Sheffield Independent*. It seems that the anonymous woman, now named as Mrs Adams, had not been teaching arithmetic but had been in fact teaching religious instruction to the children. The letter stated that the Guardians:

> whilst emphasizing the need for the poor children to have spiritual instruction were aware that the schoolmaster and schoolmistress would not trouble themselves about the subject. The Poor Law arrangements do not specify that the teachers of workhouse schools teach Christian dogma and therefore there is no great impropriety in making arrangements to enable ladies such as Mrs Adams, the wife of Revd Adams, to visit the school to impart religious instruction.

One of the other Guardians, Mr Leonard, a staunch Catholic, objected strongly to this woman teaching the children. He had previously requested the chair to allow the Sisters of Mercy to attend the Pitsmoor School for the instruction of the Roman Catholic children but the chair had refused to support him in this matter. The chair pointed out to him that the country being Protestant, the workhouse institution must therefore also be considered as such. Another of the Guardians, Mr Chapman, pointed out the need for such lady visitors amounted to 'a censure of the Guardians for failing to provide religious instructions for the children who were in their care'. He pointed out that 'supposing the lady visitors are allowed to give religious instruction to the children, wouldn't that give a right to another set of religious women from another denomination to attend and give instruction also?' The chair pointed out that the Guardians had the right to censor the schoolmaster and schoolmistress, but had no power over lady visitors. The Board of Guardians was, not for the first time, completely divided on this question. When a motion was put forward to allow the lady visitors to continue to attend the school children as previously, no one offered to second the motion and 'the proposition fell to the ground'.

It had been noted that in the previous ten years the schoolmaster and mistress had changed six or seven times and the Guardians agreed that this would not benefit the children's education. Combining this with the hostility towards the master had increased the mismanagement of the school. The Poor Law Board declared that in order to remedy this, the school at Pitsmoor must now be a completely separate establishment from Kelham Street and must be enlarged in order to have its own master and matron, superintendent, porter and Medical Officer. Not surprisingly, the Guardians disagreed, and in February

1859 informed the Poor Law Board that in their opinion an assistant matron and the schoolmaster and schoolmistress under the supervision of Mr and Mrs Rogers were adequate provision for the care of the children. The following week they discussed the issue once more and resolved that:

> to elect other officers is uncalled for. The children are separated from other paupers and are well looked after. The children are healthier and their religious and moral needs are being attended to. The Guardians are satisfied with the present master and matron so far and can see no room for any accommodation for extra staff. The Guardians are not prepared to enlarge the building further.

The chair instructed the clerk to send this resolution to the Poor Law Board, and he could not refrain from commenting that he knew of 'no other body of men whose public conduct was more deserving of censure'.

Unfortunately, however, the Poor Law authorities were proved right, and it was not long before the Pitsmoor school was finally deemed to be too small. The desperate need to enlarge the building was discussed ten months later in December 1859. At that time the Pitsmoor schools held ninety-eight children, but with just a few alterations the site could be made to accommodate 150. Within the larger establishment accommodation would be made for a master, matron and a porter, and they took up the suggestion made by the Poor Law Board. Some of the committee felt that the addition of a small wing to the Pitsmoor School could provide all the necessary accommodation at very low cost with the same outcome. But the chair pointed out that as the whole town of Sheffield felt the importance of properly looking after pauper children there would be no opposition about the costs of £800. The Guardian's clerk, requested the Guardians to appoint a separate master and matron to Pitsmoor workhouse at the earliest opportunity for several reasons:

> The children suffered great inconvenience and discomfort in having to come to the workhouse and back several times a day.
> There was not a good understanding between Mr Rogers and the schoolmaster.
> The late unpleasantness between the Protestants and the Catholics had arisen mainly from the want of a master and matron.

By 6 October 1860 it was reported that 'the work at the schools had been completed'. The chair told the other Guardians that the schools now 'consisted of beautiful rooms and there was no doubt how satisfactory it was'.

Despite the Guardians' satisfaction with the school, the Poor Law Board informed them on 23 July 1862 that they had concerns over the employment of workhouse paupers at the school. They also criticised the inadequacy of 'the want of day accommodation and the small size of the yards for the children to play'. The chair acidly commented that it was a pity that the Poor Law Board, who had 'so much important business on their hands in looking after the starving and destitute people of Lancashire and other counties, should trouble themselves with matters of this kind'. This was a reference to the Lancashire Cotton famine, which, due to the American Civil War, had been unable to export the raw cotton. As a result, thousands of workers in the cotton trades of Lancashire were out of work and were forced to apply for relief. The Guardians resolved that the following resolution be sent to the Poor Law Board:

That the accommodation of the school at Pitsmoor is such that met the approval of the Poor Law Board at the period of their alteration in 1860 when the plans for the whole accommodation for day and nights wards was submitted… and given their sanction.

That the day and night accommodation is the same now as when approved by the Poor Law Board. The Guardians therefore believe that the day accommodation must be amply sufficient, being in strict accordance with plans sanctioned.

That the schoolrooms are larger than the generality of free schools for the same number of children and that a large dining hall being attached, other accommodation appears quite unnecessary, especially as the children enjoy remarkably good health. At this present time out of 172 children only 10 are ill and those with trifling complaints.

That the yards although not large are larger than the average playground attached to the majority of free schools and appear sufficient in size, especially as the children have a large garden to work in and constantly walk in the country which is of easy access from the schools.

That with respect of the paupers acting as servants the Guardians believe the system works well. The children know nothing of them being paupers and the union is saved an unnecessary outlay and the paupers are well employed in occupations likely to engender habits of industry and independence.

The Guardians, while greatly obliged to Mr Mainwaring and the Poor Law Board, believe from the intimate knowledge they have of the schools at Pitsmoor they are quite capable of judging the success of the systems pursued and the accommodation provided. Should the Guardians find alteration or additions desirable they will at once, when trade is such as to justify them in spending the ratepayer's money for such purposes, request of the Poor Law Board the liberty to make them.

Mr Saunders reported on 22 March 1865 that 'the children were much healthier and happier than they had been at the Kelham Street workhouse, a change which other members of the public had taken note of'. He told them that on the previous day the children had been walking through the town accompanied by the schoolmaster when a man stopped him on Castle Street and told him:

Those children bring great credit on the Guardians; they look so healthy and clean and are so nicely dressed. Dirt, rags, squalor and neglect were associated with pauper children, but the children in the Sheffield Union Schools would compare with the children in any philanthropic institution in the town.

Castle Street and Waingate, where the workhouse children were praised.

He also told the Board that the children were supplied with good food, poles had been erected in the playground for them to play on and every means had been taken to make them healthy and happy. Despite these assurances, however, there had been reports of lack of supervision for the children. In May 1865 it was brought to the Guardian's attention that the children were allowed to go into the town of Sheffield without the teachers. Fifteen of these children had recently been found in a public house on Furnace Hill into which they had been 'enticed and dressed up and made to dance and sing for the amusement of the customers'. They were paid a few pennies but the Guardians were concerned about their moral welfare and resolved that the schoolmaster and schoolmistress take them out on activities twice a week to prevent this happening again. Matters did not improve, and it seems that there was further criticism from the Poor Law Board in March 1869, when it was reported that it was impossible for one master to control 116 children and that an assistant teacher had to be appointed. There is no mention of this appointment and by June the Guardians requested that the schoolmaster select a number of boys and girls to act as monitors.

The schoolteachers must have been sorely frustrated by the constant criticisms of the school and the long hours which they had to serve. The frustration which they felt may have been the reason for some very cruel behaviour by the master to some of his charges. One of the Pitsmoor teachers, Mr Turner, was criticised on 22 December 1859. In his statement the master, Mr Rogers, claimed that he had heard an altercation as he left the dining hall and returned to find that a mother, Mrs Mary Costello, had been informed by her daughter of the schoolmaster's cruel treatment: it seems that William Costello, aged five and a half, had asked permission to go to the toilet and, on being refused, had wet himself. The schoolmaster instructed him to clean the floor with a floor cloth, and had then rubbed the child's face with it, taking off some of the skin and causing his face to bleed. The mother removed her child from the school. She also struck the teacher, who

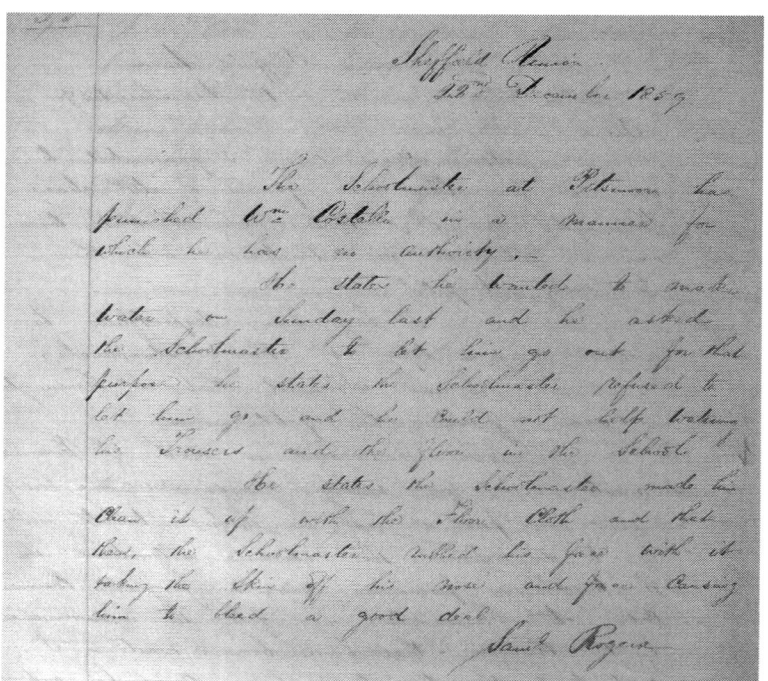

Mr Rogers' report on the treatment of William Costello.

promptly called a constable. The teacher was requested to appear before the Guardians at the next Board meeting and to bring his punishment book with him. The book revealed that the punishment had been unrecorded. The Guardians informed him that according to the General Consolidated Order all punishments of the children had to be recorded in his punishment book.

The following month yet another case appeared before the Guardians regarding a boy called Storey. The schoolmaster wrote a letter to the Board and agreed that he had hit the boy. He told them that the boy put out his arm to ward off the blow, and as a result the schoolmaster's blow landed on his head instead of his shoulders. However, he stated that when he saw blood coming from his head 'he stopped the punishment and sent the boy to have his head washed'. Another schoolmaster was forced to resign following an allegation of 'cruelly beating a boy' on 20 February 1878. These cases indicate the sorts of punishments inflicted on the children of the Pitsmoor School.

However, not all workhouse teachers were the same. The *Sheffield Independent* of January 1876 printed an account of an unnamed pauper kindly remembering a former schoolmaster of Pitsmoor School named Mr T. Westenholm. The teacher was described as 'a middle aged but kindly looking person' who was:

untiring in his zeal to fit us for the duties of life. He was a musician, artist, horticulturist and botanist. A true lover of nature, he would in the early spring and summer take us to the woods and awake admiration in our breasts. When walking out the bystanders' expressions were more often complimentary than otherwise. These comments fell on our ears. 'See there t'workhouse childer' and 'they don't look as if they were clammed' [starved]. The schoolmaster would be engaged in conversation with the children which was always his custom when we were out for a walk. At home he would beguile the evenings with his violin, learning us to sing some new piece or sketch some scene we had visited so our surrounding should tend to develop rather than retard latent genius.

By 1848 the government recognised that workhouse teachers needed to have a better education, and they paid grants to the Guardians for those who gained certificates in competency. These certificates listed the level of education for the teachers and also the number of children they were now able to teach. The standard of teaching in the workhouse immediately became more professional, and hopefully matters steadily improved.

There had been many debates in the national press about the need to teach workhouse children. Some people thought it a complete waste of time, whilst others felt it would be the only way that children could be taught to read and write. This would lead to better chances of employment and the children would no longer be a burden on ratepayers of the future. Certainly the street children of Sheffield would have no access to any kind of education unless they entered the workhouse. Supporters of the workhouse system pointed out that it gave paupers admittance to two advantages which they had previously been unable to access: teachers and an education, and workhouse Medical Officers and improved health conditions.

seven

Medical Officers of Health

Sheffield during the Victorian era was not a healthy town to live in, and as industries thrived, less thought was given to what effect this was having on the poor people of the town. The unsanitary state of Sheffield was described in the *Sheffield and Rotherham Independent* on 7 October 1861, where it reported:

> spoil heaps or ash pits are scattered around the town where the scavengers would add all the refuse from the streets; one is positioned under a railway arch on Victoria Road. The Duke of Norfolk has his own 'hillock of filth' where are collected the sweeping of his markets and properties where it is reported that children were playing with offal and one little chap was seen chewing on a decaying leek. Produce from the shops are trodden underfoot leaving a thick greasy crust on most streets of the town and the channels crossing and the footpaths catches the liquid manure which runs from many houses and stables.

These were the conditions in which Sheffield people made as good an existence as they were able to. Sanitary conditions in both Kelham Street and Fir Vale workhouses must have been appalling due to the amounts of people living there as toilet facilities were known to be basic and overworked. It was not until April of 1893, following a recommendation from the Medical Officer, that water closets were installed in the workhouse instead of the communal ash pits and privies of the period.

Before the Poor Law Acts there is little evidence of how medical services were supplied to the paupers. It is supposed that a medical man was attached to the workhouses on West Bar and on Kelham Street before the Act, but many of the ailments of the poor would have been treated by nurses. These early nurses were generally paid little or no wages and many of them would have been paupers themselves. Not until the 1834 Act were Medical Officers appointed with the sanction of the Poor Law Commissioners to take care of the health needs of the workhouse inmates. It was agreed by the early Guardians that there would be one Medical Officer resident in the workhouse and others would be appointed to the districts to take care of the paupers out of the workhouse. Relieving officers who

Victorian housing in Sheffield, with sewage accumulating in the yard.

identified medical concerns would send an order for a medical man to attend to the patient and dispense medicine – or sometimes spirits, which were thought to aid recovery – in the form of 'extras'. In some cases paupers would have to be brought into the workhouse hospital to be cared for. There was always concern that bringing sick people into such a large building would spread infection, particularly during the many epidemics which were virulent in confined and industrial towns and cities. These epidemics were frightening to our modern eyes. On 8 July 1832, just three years after the workhouse on Kelham Street had been opened, an outbreak of cholera hit Sheffield. It proved to be devastating before its course had been run. By the 21st the health authorities for the town reported that they had some twenty-five cases of cholera, resulting in ten deaths. A dispensary in the Park had been opened, although there was no reliable medicine with which to treat these patients – and the death toll grew. Despite the risk of contagion, on 26 July a public meeting was called to discuss the situation and to make provision for an isolation hospital for cholera victims. The overseers of the town immediately advanced £1,000 for accommodation to be made for these patients. Then the numbers grew alarmingly, as the following list indicates:

Date	No. of Cases	Deaths
28 July	50	24
11 August	352	122
18 August	630	207
25 August	895	299
1 September	1086	342
8 September	1187	350
15 September	1236	368
22 September	1263	376
10 October	1306	390

Finally, in November, the disease began to come under control, and the town took up its former life once more. By 5 November the total number of cases had been 1,347, and out of those 402 people had died. Cholera was no respecter of people in high places. One of the victims had been a master cutler named John Blake, who died at the height of the epidemic. All the bodies were buried on a small piece of ground near to Clay Wood and two years later a memorial for the victims of the epidemic was erected in Monument Gardens on Norfolk Road. There was little understanding about the dreadful sanitary conditions of the privies, many of which leaked into the water supply. Living in those kinds of conditions resulted in a further outbreak of cholera on 22 July 1849, and by 22 August it was once again on the increase. The only solution the town could offer was prayer, and on 28 September a 'Day of Humiliation' was observed in the town. On the same day, it was noted, Mr Henry Bower of Wicker Foundry died; he was the first of four people to die in the same house. Thankfully, however, by 20 October the epidemic was lessening. On 15 November 1849 a 'Day of Thanksgiving' was declared for the cessation of the disease.

We know from notes written by the master and by reports copied into the letter book that the resident Medical Officer in the Kelham Street workhouse in September 1847 was a Mr J. Deakin. On 14 September the master wrote a note to him asking him to attend a patient. He wrote: 'Sarah Ann Yeardley is taken suddenly ill and requires your earliest attention. I shall be much obliged if you will see the child soon. We do not know what the matter is with her.'

The following month the Medical Officer was a man called Benjamin Micklethwaite. The master sent a request for Mr Micklethwaite to attend a case on 19 October. This was a woman called Mary Cox. Mary had given birth without the doctor attending, but complications had arisen and she 'urgently' required attention. Unfortunately, the poor woman died the same night. As it was also the master's duty to let the superintendent of police, Mr Raynor, know when a person died in the workhouse, he later informed him that the same patient:

Mary Cox, aged 29, and her husband and children were admitted here on the 16th instant and was in a state of exhaustion through fever and they were taken straight to the fever ward. Yesterday she was delirious, and this morning she was prematurely delivered of a still-born child and the mother died shortly afterwards. Dr Micklethwaite saw her previous to her death.

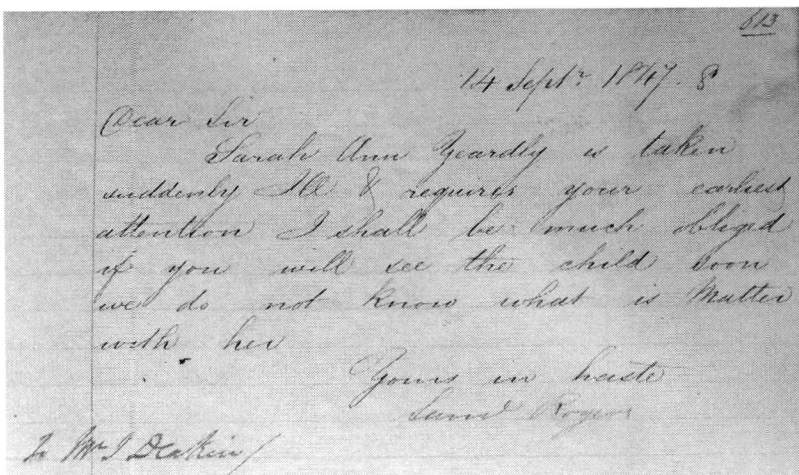

Letter to the
Medical Officer
regarding Sarah
Ann Yeardley.

The Medical Officer or the master had to let the superintendent of police know whether the patient had been seen by a doctor prior to the death: if a patient died of an unknown cause the coroner would have to be informed, and an inquest and post-mortem held. Another note was sent to him from a George Woodcock, asking him to visit a man in his lodging house in the town who was said to be dangerously ill. The Medical Officer duly noted that the man, John Gillis, was 'non compos mentis' – a medical term for deranged – and he was taken immediately to the workhouse and from there to the asylum.

The resident Medical Officer would live in the workhouse and would probably be in attendance for much of the day. His duties covered all the paupers in the workhouse from their arrival to their discharge. Paupers who arrived at the workhouse would be examined by him, and if he saw any signs of disease they would be sent to the hospital. He also had to report to the Guardians on a regular basis any sanitary defects in the workhouse as well as on the health of the paupers. There was also a surgery at the workhouse for poor people to attend themselves. There was no doubt that he would work extremely hard, particularly when the workhouse was overcrowded. Medical officers in the districts were summoned by an order from the relieving officer and they would visit the patient in their own home and supply medicine or extras as they required. They would be expected to attend promptly to any order given to them and it was a common complaint that there was a delay in their attendance. Any complaint was taken seriously by the Guardians and investigated fully.

Such a complaint was made against one of the Medical Officers, Mr Atkin, in October 1856 by the family of Thomas Crowder. An article in the local newspaper had outlined the allegation and Mr Atkin appeared before the Guardians to offer his explanation. It seems that Mr Crowder had suffered three attacks of apoplexy and he died during the third attack. Mr Atkin pointed out to the Guardians that it was such a virulent attack that even if he had been there in the house, there was nothing he could have done. When he reached the house he was informed by the widow that her husband was dead and she requested a death certificate. He wrote on the back of the certificate what he thought was the cause of death and stated that he had not seen the deceased for the information of the coroner. In reply to the allegation that he had not attended to his patient soon enough, he said that he had not assumed from the manner of the daughter who had summoned him that the case was urgent, so he elected to see him on the following day. As an example, he told the Guardians that very morning he had received two 'urgent cases' to visit from the relieving officers. The first one was an old woman who was allegedly dying. When he arrived at the house the woman was sitting reading and was unaware that the Medical Officer had been sent for. When he arrived at the second case, his patient, an old man, was asleep, and he had the greatest difficulty in waking him. The only reason he had been called was because the old man had toothache. He would have been quite capable of walking to the surgery on his own, had he so required. The Guardians were quite happy with this explanation, and the chair thanked Mr Atkin for his attendance.

A further case of neglect was put before the Guardians on 31 March 1860 when another Medical Officer, Mr Le Tall, was accused of neglecting a patient called Sarah Lister who he had not seen for several weeks before her death. She was in so much pain that her husband had been forced to pay for another surgeon to attend her. She had chronic disease of the heart and he was in the habit of going to see her without an order. He told the Guardians that the last time he had seen her she had told him that she didn't need to see him any more. He agreed with the daughter that they would send for him if she took worse, and so he had no knowledge that she was ill again. He had received an order from the relieving officer Mr Head late in the day and was unable to see her that night. The following morning he visited to find her dead. Once again the Guardians were happy with his explanation, and he was exonerated.

On both these occasions the Guardians had defended their Medical Officer, but three years later they seemed to go to war with them. Following an outbreak of smallpox in August 1863, the Medical Officers made their report to the Guardians: from 1 May to 30 June 1863, they said, there had been 226 cases of smallpox, and of these 19 sufferers had died. The Guardians asked the Medical Officers to supply them with information regarding the number of deaths in each of their districts from smallpox in an attempt to find ways of halting the infection. The Medical Officers referred the Guardians to their medical books (which they supplied to the Board every week). They said the books should provide all the information that they required. The Guardians complained that the handwriting of the different Medical Officers was unreadable, and they were unable to gain the necessary information from the books. Then the matter got completely out of hand: a formal letter was sent to the Guardians signed by five Medical Officers and reiterating their claim that the information could be found in their books, and stating that they had sent details of the matter to the Poor Law Commissioners in London. The chair was incensed by this: he felt that as the officers were employed by the Guardians, and their salary paid by them, supplying information was the least the Medical Officers could do. One of the Guardians, Mr Hallam, noted that 'their conduct is most ungracious and uncourteous'. The chair remarked that: 'he would give them to the first of the month to hand over the returns required as it was impossible to extract the information from the books as the writing of the medical men and the peculiar Latin/English language used made them impossible to decipher'.

Letter printed in newspapers from the Medical Officers.

"We, the undersigned medical officers of the Sheffield Union, beg to acknowledge the receipt of a communication from your clerk, dated the 7th August instant, in reference to a resolution passed at the meeting of your board on the 15th July last, and we beg to state that, in reply to the request contained in the resolution referred to, we forwarded a letter on the 28th July last, addressed to your board, in which we stated that the 'medical relief book furnishes all the information which your resolution requests.'

"As we have not received a reply to that letter, we have considered it advisable to submit the facts of the case to the Poor Law Commissioners in London, so as to ascertain from them whether we are required to furnish the monthly report you apply for, and if so, the precise form in which it should be done.—We are, gentlemen, your obedient servants,

"JOHN SYKES.
"HERBERT F. WALKER.
"ELIJAH BARKER.
"F. GRIFFITHS.
"HENRY ALLANSON, M.D.
"S. ARDEN.
"Sheffield, August 12th, 1863."

The Guardians also sent a request to the Poor Law Board asking them to compel the Medical Officers to supply the required information. The Board replied that 'under article 205 of the General Consolidated Order it does not empower the Guardians to demand returns from the Medical Officers in this fashion'. The chair was outraged, complaining that as a result of their defiance the Guardians couldn't be held responsible for the spreading of the sickness in the town. He stated that the Poor Law Board should give the Guardians greater powers to prevent officers refusing to do what the Guardians demanded. He was then forced to let the matter drop.

The relationship between the Medical Officers and the Guardians did not improve. In the run up to the election of the Guardians in April 1864 a handbill had been produced, supposedly written by some of the Medical Officers of the Kelham Street workhouse. The handbill stated that some of the existing Guardians were 'practicing grinding tyranny' towards the poor and 'showing partiality in issuing of union contracts'. The handbill called upon the working classes not to vote for three of the Guardians, Messrs Saunders, Hallam and Muddiman. One of the Guardians claimed that some of the Medical Officers had paid men to vote against the three men. The Guardians were naturally incensed, and resolved that the clerk write to Dr Allanson, Mr H.J. Walker, Dr Griffiths and Dr S. Arden to ascertain the correctness of the report. He was instructed to point out to these officers that the Poor Law Commissioners regarded the interference of the election of union officers to be a very serious offence, one which could lead to immediate dismissal. One of the other Guardians, Mr Youdan, opposed this course of action, advising his colleagues not to bring a petty squabble into public notice. However, he was overruled, and the letters were sent. The Board then discussed the amount of extras claimed by Dr Allanson for a recent confinement case which had been disputed by the Guardians, and they refused to pay all of it. It seems that in such cases Mr Allenson had to attend the patient two or three days after the confinement, but on this occasion he had sent a student in his place. Dr Allenson was brought before the Guardians and, after a heated discussion, was told that the Board was unable to pay the extra and due to the length of time any payments would now have to be sanctioned by the Poor Law Board. The chair advised Dr Allenson to take the amount that the Board had allowed if he wanted the money. Dr Allenson stated 'very heatedly' that: 'he did not want the money, it was the principle that wanted settling. That if he did want for any money the chairman would be the last person he would apply to for it.'

The chair repeated the offer, saying that he thought the Medical Officer might need the money 'after his expenditure in the recent elections'. Dr Allanson replied hotly: 'Sir, if you come to my house I should there be able to say to you all I would like to say. In this room I cannot'. The chair reminded him that it was only from the goodwill of the Guardians that he could get a penny of his bill. Dr Allanson then left the room and the Board continued with their business. By December 1864 the relationship between the Medical Officer and the Guardians had not improved, and they were still refusing to submit returns to the Guardians. The local newspaper reported 'this interminable dispute' when the Medical Officers accounts were once more laid before the Guardians. The chair stated that:

> the Guardians have no personal feelings in refusing to pay the Medical Officers' accounts in dispute. Much less are they activated by any wish to punish the Medical Officers for their want of courtesy in refusing to supply the Guardians with the returns. They are simply desirous that sick people are treated properly.

However, Mr Allenson's sloppy paperwork resulted in a request from the Guardians to give him twenty-eight days' notice in February 1865. It seems that instead of inserting the patients' addresses on the forms, Mr Allenson had simply written 'Sheffield'. The clerk had written to him previously on the subject, but Mr Allenson refused to conform. The chair insisted that: 'he had shown no respect to the Guardians and referred to them as "fellows". For months we have been antagonized by the Medical Officers who refused our requests and it has interfered with the smooth running of the union.'

However, on this occasion no one would second the motion, so it 'fell to the ground'. Five months later, in July 1865, feelings were still running high when one of the Guardians, Mr Jackson, said that 'the time had come to put an end to the strife between the Medical Officers and the Guardians. Dr Allenson's conduct has been most defiant to the Board and they would show him that they possessed some power to regulate it'. This time the voting was unanimous, and twenty-eight days' notice was sent. It was agreed that another Medical Officer was to be appointed. The Guardians may have got rid of one of their Medical Officers, but ten years later they had to deal with two complaints against two Medical Officers who were both suspended in the same month.

A complaint had been made against another Medical Officer, Mr Skinner, by a patient named Mrs Cauldwell in January of 1875, and the Guardians had no option but to suspend him for neglect of duty. When he was summoned before the Guardians to explain, he told them that his attendances were recorded in his medical book. However, when the book was produced he admitted that he had completed the entries and 'marked the book lately'. He also astonished the Guardians by telling them that he had ordered beef tea and wine when he had thought there was no necessity because it was 'on Alderman Searle's recommendation alone'. The chair, Mr Searle, rose to his feet to express his indignation at this remark and completely denied that he had ordered anything. Mr Skinner further informed the Board that when he went to Mrs Cauldwell's house her sister, Mrs Dawson, had remarked that the chair had recommended wine. Once again the Boardroom fell into uproar: not only did the chair deny this claim, but Mrs Dawson also was brought before the Guardians and stated that she had said no such thing. An official enquiry was held by Mr Basil Cane for the Local Government Board on 4 February 1875. Mr Skinner once again denied that he had neglected Mrs Cauldwell. However, the Local Government Board found that there was no charge to answer, and felt that Mr Skinner should be reinstated. Some of the Guardians felt that Mr Skinner had lied to the enquiry and requested that another investigation be held into the matter, but a letter was received from the Local Government Board refusing to hold another enquiry and there the matter was left.

The same month a further case of neglect had been brought to the Guardian's attention. It involved another of the Medical Officers, a Mr Packman. On 11 February, an allegation was brought from Mrs Newsome of Creswick Walk, Pond Hill, alleging that Mr Packman had neglected her children, who were suffering from whooping cough. By the time Mr Packman arrived the baby was dead. When Mr Packman was brought before the Guardians to give an explanation, he informed them that he was incensed at the charge and he was dismissed from the room. It was resolved that both Medical Officers, Packman and Skinner, be suspended. The Guardians received a letter from the Local Government Board the following week declaring that they had looked into the alleged case of neglect by Mr Packman and felt that the child, suffering as it was from whooping cough, did not require frequent medical attendances. They offered their opinion that the suspension should be removed. One of the Guardians, Mr Shipman, told the room that in his view they were in a 'bonny mess':

What a glorious thing it is to be a Guardian, to do just what a Board in London said they should do! What was the use of being elected by the ratepayers? When he was sent to the Board of Guardians they imagined that he and the other members of the Board were to use their own judgment in looking after the interests of the ratepayers generally, but it seems they have no power to do that.

But the Guardians had no option but to remove the suspensions. Only a year later Mr Packman was complaining about the amount of orders he had from the receiving officers for medical attention. He told the Guardians that he was receiving over twenty-five calls a week, as well as attending approximately 120 cases on the same orders for weeks and months. He warned that if some check was not put on these orders he would be attending half the population of Sheffield.

The Medical Officers during times of epidemics were responsible for working closely with the Guardians to prevent further infection. Arguments were put on one side following an outbreak of cholera in London in 1866, which the groups feared would soon be at Sheffield. The newspapers reported the strategies with which the Guardians and the Medical Officers sought to prevent the disease affecting the town. The chair reported to his colleagues that 'in the last two months more than 5,000 tons of night soil had been removed to Lincolnshire and other depots where it was deodorized'. The Health Committee had all rivers and goits cleaned out, at a cost of £300; the sewers and rivers

Poor housing conditions were endemic in the city.

had already been cleaned out by the heavy rain which had been experienced. There had also been many requests for free lime from the householders of the town. The relieving officers and Medical Officers were given free 'lime tickets' for any pauper that applied for them. It was thought that lime could be spread on privies and rubbish tips to prevent the spread of cholera, which was at the time thought to be airborne. In reality, however, the epidemic flourished because of the poor living conditions and sanitation in the area. It was further resolved that free medicine was to be provided at all hours and that if any cases of excessive diarrhoea were brought to the attention of the Medical Officers then a nurse would be sent to the patient's house, and good food supplied to the patient. Large posters advising householders what to do to keep their houses clean and free from infection had been erected in the town. The posters recommended that: 'to prevent getting cholera householders had to keep themselves as clean as possible and allow no dirt to remain in the house. All windows should be kept open and not much fruit eaten. Too much intoxicating liquor should be avoided and diseased meat and fish should be thrown away.'

By September of 1866, Mr Skinner's report for the Guardians listed the very first death from cholera in the town. The deceased man was Mr Atkins, a shoemaker of Castle Street who had been taken ill on Tuesday and died the following day. Mr Skinner reported that the body had been kept in a locked room and everything from the sick room had been burnt. He told them that he had heard that there was an accumulation of rubbish at the back of the shop premises and had instructed the Nuisance Removal Inspector, Mr Chapman, not to move it but to cover it with chloride of lime. He had conferred with another Medical Officer, Mr Wiltshire, who confirmed the man had died from cholera. Mr Wiltshire told him that he had eight cases of diarrhoea in Ecclesfield – all symptomatic of cholera. Most of the patients had died the same day, and others the day after. He described one of the cases he attended, a man whom he found lying in a small cottage with a small kitchen and living room downstairs and a bedroom shared by six people. It was thought at first that the disease was caught from a grating over a drain under the kitchen window, but Mr Illingworth discovered that the source was from a 'favourite and much used well' which was polluted by drainage from a stable. In his report he stated that 'all eight fatal cases were confirmed drunkards'.

It was decided at a Board meeting on Wednesday, 30 March 1881 that they would keep Mr Hunt as the residential Medical Officer in the new workhouse at Fir Vale. Due to the large amount of patients, they agreed that he would be supported by a resident assistant Medical Officer. Another Guardian, Mr Robertshaw, disagreed with Mr Hunt's appointment, saying that during the time he had been Medical Officer Mr Hunt had barely done two hours work a day. Because of the large number of patients being admitted to the workhouse in a dying state, many were not seen for twenty-four hours. He felt it unfair that the major part of the work should therefore fall on a younger man with less experience. He felt that Dr Hunt should visit the workhouse hospital every day. After much argument and discussion it was agreed that Dr Hunt be appointed as the Medical Officer and the position of resident assistant Medical Officer was to be advertised.

By January 1882 the assistant's position had been filled by Dr Blyth – who, not surprisingly, was a man who was soon causing problems with his superiors. The matter was brought before the Guardians at a meeting of the Board on Wednesday 18 January, when the Board was informed that 'two doctors were shivering with cold on the stairs'. They were admitted, and immediately Dr Blyth stated that Dr Hunt had completed a certificate for a pauper when he had only seen her for about five minutes over a two-day period before she died. It seems that a woman named Wood had been admitted to the vagrant ward and died there. She was known to be a woman of profligate habits, and indeed had been taken to the workhouse drunk. Dr Blyth had ordered medicine for her and she was kept warm, yet despite this she died. PC Cooper was called before the Guardians and he agreed with Dr Hunt that the woman was known about the town as a drunk. Dr Hunt had made out the certificate, stating that the cause of death had been 'exhaustion', and this was what Dr Blyth objected to. Dr Blyth was forced to admit that Dr Hunt was the senior doctor, and it was pointed out to him that he should not bring complaints before the Guardians about a senior officer. The chair accused Dr Blyth of 'continually making charges which he could not support and the Guardians could not allow that sort of thing to go on. If he could not understand that Dr Hunt was the principle officer then the sooner he retired the better.'

The two doctors left the Boardroom without coming to any kind of resolution and the subject was dropped. Only a month later Mr Blyth sent a letter to the Guardians making another complaint about the lack of nurses in the hospital wards. He had drawn the Guardian's attention to the matter following a case of a patient jumping out of the window whilst being attended to by a pauper nurse. The Guardians were scathing about the letter and debated whether it should even be read out to the Board, as the complaint should have come from Mr Hunt, but as one of the Guardians, Mr Carr, pointed out, if the man had been killed by jumping out of the window an enquiry would have to be held, and if it came out in evidence that there was an insufficiency of nurses that would put the Guardians in a very difficult position. A vote was taken about whether the letter should be read or not, with five for the letter being read and seven against it. The matter was dropped, and the letter left unread.

There is no doubt that the contentious relationship between the Guardians and the Medical Officers continued. Sheffield Guardians seemed to be continually waging war with one or the other of their officers, but they were to fight some of their biggest battles with the master and matron themselves.

eight

Master and Matrons

Records indicate that one of the first workhouses established in Sheffield appears to have been a workhouse for children on the lines of an industrial school; it was already open in May 1632. The first recorded master of this workhouse was named John Pendleton; he 'came to have been the master of the workhouse', for which he was paid the sum of 7s 6d. At the same time, Nicholas Parkin was given 16s 8d 'for his monethes paie hee is to have with the children', suggesting that perhaps he was to be the new master. He was also given a cow to tend for the children the same year (which cost £3 12s 4d) and a further cow was given to him the following year (which cost £3 11s). In 1733 the master was William Lotas; in 1736 it was Thomas Braine; and in 1750 Robert Rawson gave up his post to John Lindlam, who was voted in by the majority of the freeholders of the town.

The post of master and mistress of the workhouse was traditionally held by a husband and wife team, the master being in charge of the male inmates and his wife, the matron, who in the early days was generally unpaid, the female side. The role involved being responsible, under the Guardians, for the daily running of the workhouse. The master would have to admit paupers, be responsible for the security of the house and report to the Guardians any inmate's transgressions. It was usually agreed that if one or the other died, the surviving partner would have to offer their resignation unless the Guardians agreed to keep them on. It would be tedious to list the names of all the masters of Sheffield workhouse even if they were available, so I have tended to concentrate on just a few. It was announced in June 1844 that Mr Samuel Rogers, aged forty-two, formerly of Chard Union workhouse and before that master at Redruth in Cornwall, was elected to be the master of Sheffield workhouse. He and his wife would commence their duties on 26 July 1844. The position of master carried a lot of weight, and it was commented at his death thirteen years later that 'in the previous past the Sheffield Guardians had rarely visited the house, so the management of it was in his power'. Although he had managed his duties to the Guardians' satisfaction, it was commented at the same time that 'sometimes he was more dominant than was required'. The reason for this is quite easily found. Many of the workhouse masters and matrons saw the inmates as their servants, which no doubt added to their feelings of infallibility. Certainly from the records it appears that both Mr and Mrs Rogers were arrogant people, intent on getting their own way.

Little record is left of the early few years of Mr Rogers' mastership of the Kelham Street workhouse, and what there is may be found in the workhouse letter books (which date from 1847–1861). Part of the master's duties was to notify relatives when one of the workhouse inmates was not expected to live. In September of 1847 it was Mr Rogers's duty to notify such a relative and possibly give them a chance to see that person before they died. He wrote to Mr Bennett of George Street, Stockport: 'Sir, I am directed to inform you that your mother Elizabeth Bennett is very ill and that she is not likely to recover. I am Sir, Your Obedient Servant, Samuel Rogers.'

It was common that Mr Rogers would notify the relatives the same day. In some cases he would comment on the help that they gave in the workhouse, as we see in the next note, written later the same month, sent to a Mr Richard Eccles: 'I have now the duty to inform you that your brother William Eccles died here this evening about 7.30 p.m. It is our intention to inter the corpse at the Sheffield General Cemetery on Saturday next at 4 p.m. In sending you the information I feel strongly urged to record my feelings on the subject. That in the death of William Eccles I have lost a very honest and faithful servant.'

It would seem that certain persons were sent to the workhouse not because they were destitute but because they were criminals. A letter was sent from the mayor, Edward Vickers, to Mr Rogers in November 1847 about a man named Martin Magrian. The mayor told him that the man had been before the Bench on many occasions for felony. He declared that, 'I think the best mode of disposing of him would be in the workhouse,' informing Mr Rogers that his father was not in a position to pay for his maintenance. There is no mention of what the Guardians felt about this arrangement, but as the instructions had come from the mayor they were not in a position to argue.

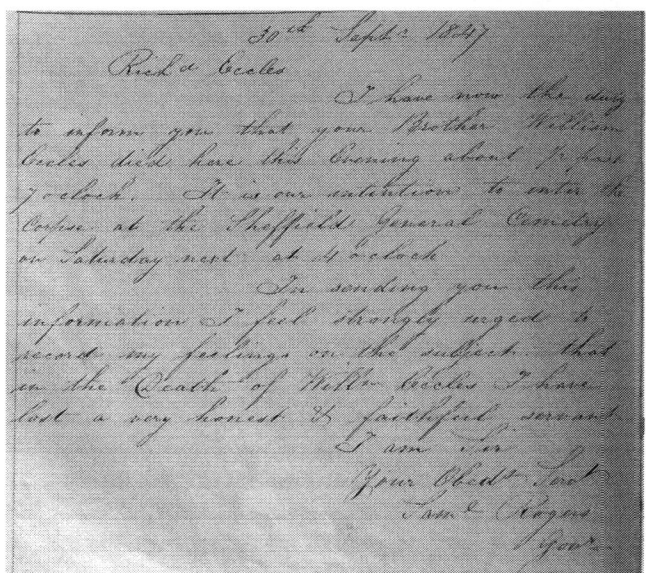

Letter written from Mr Rogers to Richard Eccles regarding his brother's death.

As Sheffield was such a large workhouse, there was a role for an assistant master and an advertisement for such a post appeared in the *Sheffield Daily Telegraph* on Tuesday, 30 September 1856. The advert stated that the Sheffield Guardians of the poor needed a young man 'fully competent to keep the workhouse books required by the Poor Law Board and other books that the Guardians may from time to time direct to be kept'. The person appointed, a Mr Huntsman, was before long going to cause the master a lot of grief. On Thursday, 16 July 1857 the local newspapers reported that Mr Huntsman had revealed that there were serious errors in the workhouse books. A 'long discussion followed', and the books were brought for the Guardians' inspection. Mr Huntsman alleged that a woman named Margaret Grant, who had been discharged from the workhouse on 25 February the previous year, was still listed in the books as receiving rations up to 16 May. A second case, involving a man known as William Stringer, was found to be similar: according to the books he also received rations up to the previous day. This error was proved by comparison with the porter's books, which showed that he had left several weeks previously. Mr Rogers was brought into the room, but was unable to reply to the Guardians' enquiries, and the books were referred to the auditors. On 28 July Mr Huntsman told the Guardians in another letter that he had spoken to Mr Mainwaring, the Poor Law Inspector, concerning the irregularities in the books, and that the Inspector had advised him to inform the Poor Law Board in London. The Board replied that he would first need to supply further evidence of the errors by providing a distinct statement on each case. In order to fulfil the request, he asked the Guardians for access to the master's books. He was granted this access but, as one of the Guardian's prophesized, 'this matter was going to turn into a real mare's nest'. He was not wrong!

On Wednesday, 9 August 1857 the Guardians received another letter from Mr Huntsman complaining of a row that had developed between himself and Mr Rogers, who had accused him of dishonesty and of betraying his trust and called him a 'viper', a 'scorpion' and a 'cut throat'. He gathered up all the books that Mr Huntsman had been inspecting and took them away. He then imperiously commanded him to do his own job and make sure the accounts were up-to-date and 'to do that and nothing else'. At this point Mr Rogers was brought into the Boardroom and the letter read out to him. He nodded in agreement and stated that the facts were true. The books he had taken were 'the ones the Medical Officer required for a report he was writing', but he denied using bad language towards his assistant. Mr Huntsman was then summoned. The chair asked Mr Huntsman how long he had been in the employ of the workhouse, and he replied about eight months. It was pointed out to him that some of the errors had occurred before he had been employed; he agreed, but pointed out that he could not balance his books due to the errors. He was sent out whilst the Guardians discussed the matter with the master. The master told them that Mr Huntsman was constantly late in doing the accounts, and that he had frequently had to do the accounts himself to make sure they were ready for the Guardians' meeting. He stated that the previous assistant master, Mr Pringle, had always kept the accounts scrupulously. Mr Rogers said the complaints had only come to light since the master had words with his assistant about the fact that he had left the workhouse without his permission. Mr Huntsman was reprimanded, and no doubt the Guardians hoped that would put an end to the matter.

Two months later, on Wednesday, 7 October 1857, the master reported that Mr Huntsman had left the workhouse once again without permission. He had gone out on the previous Friday at 7 p.m., and returned back on Saturday at 9 a.m. He had gone out again on the Saturday night about 7 p.m. and not returned until Monday morning at 8 a.m. As a consequence, the quarterly returns had not been completed. The Board agreed that this could not go on and asked the master if he knew of a replacement should they agree to discharge the assistant master. He told them that he knew a young man who was very efficient and highly recommended. Once again Mr Huntsman was brought into the Boardroom and asked why he had left without permission; he explained that he had had some very important business to deal with – but refrained from stating what the important business had been. The chair asked, 'was he aware that no one should leave the workhouse without the express permission of the master?' He told them he 'didn't know that'. He claimed that he returned quite prepared to do the accounts, but that Mr Rogers wouldn't let him have the books, and further that 'he should never have them again'. He was asked to retire and the master told the Guardians that his conduct was having a detrimental effect on the other officers of the workhouse who would be tempted to follow his example. The Guardians had no option but to take a vote on whether Mr Huntsman should be dismissed. With four Guardians voting against and four voting for his dismissal the chair was forced to give a casting vote, and it was agreed that he be dismissed with a month's pay and, no doubt to Mr Rogers' complete relief, an advertisement for a new assistant master was inserted in the local newspaper the following week.

However, it was not long before Mr Rogers found another target for his venom. Mr William Williamson was an assistant in one of the male wards at the workhouse. On several occasions he had approached the Guardians for an advance in his wages, requests which were usually denied. A letter from him to Mr Rogers was sent in October 1858 regarding the assistant matron, Mrs Morgan, declared that 'if she doesn't keep her impertinence to herself... he would make her'. Relationships between himself and Mr Rogers broke down to such an extent that he begged him in May 1859 to 'put everything behind them', before asking Mr Rogers for a reference. Mr Rogers' reference was perhaps not quite what Mr Williamson expected: the master wrote: 'My opinion of Mr Williamson is that he is a conceited, disaffected man and I cannot but feel a satisfaction that he is leaving here. I hope that he will do better for himself. SR.' Not only did Mr Rogers give Mr Williamson a terrible reference – he copied the letter out into the book for all eternity.

Mr Rogers died on 23 March 1861, and the Guardians offered their sympathies to Mrs Rogers. It was reported in the local newspaper that he had died, aged sixty-two, 'from a variety of illnesses, but the main cause was pneumonia'. The Guardians agreed that he had been an excellent master of the workhouse and they commented that 'it would be a long time before they found someone like him'. Although it was protocol that the matron be asked to resign on the death of her husband, it was resolved that an advert was to be inserted in the local newspaper for a master. Mr Westcoe was appointed and it was agreed that Mrs Rogers could continue in her role as matron, a matter that would divide the Guardians as well as the officers in the workhouse. Events would show that Mrs Sarah Rogers felt that she could not only take on the Guardians of Sheffield but also the Poor Law Board itself.

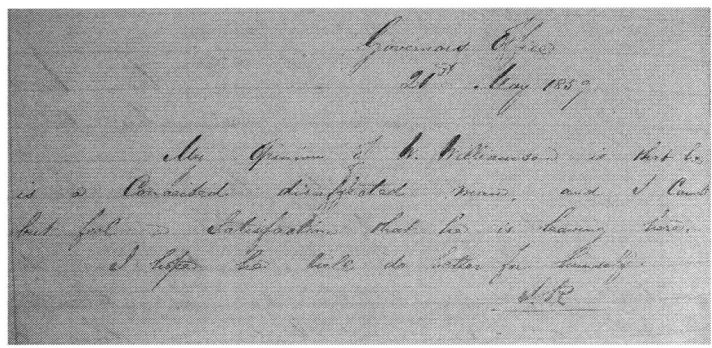

Mr Rogers' reference for William Williamson.

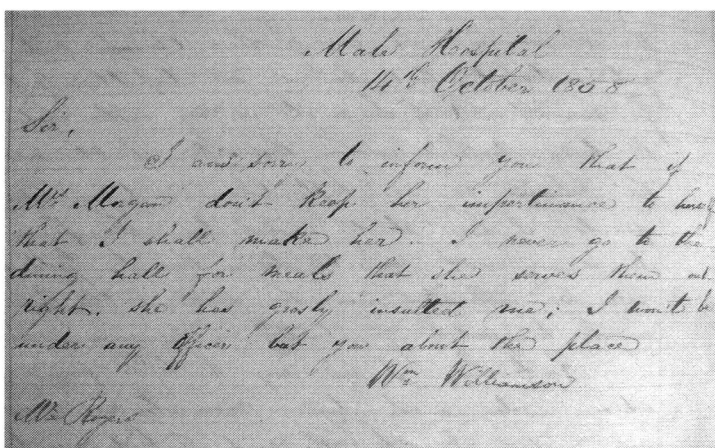

Letter from William Williamson requesting that Mrs Morgan 'keep her impertinence to herself'.

The first rumblings of complaint were brought against Mrs Rogers in November 1861, the same year as the death of her husband. It seems that the chair of the Guardians had been in the porter's lodge when one of the inmates stated that she had been to a funeral. She was dressed in ordinary workhouse clothing, yet in May 1861 an order for 40 yards of black material and three mourning shawls had been provided for the inmates as funeral attire. The chair asked where these provisions were and Mrs Rogers told them that she could only find about 12 yards of the black material and had no idea what had happened to the rest of it. She suggested that it had been stolen out of the stores. The chair asked the visiting committee to look into the matter and they began a systematic search of the workhouse. When they inspected the cellar, to which only Mrs Rogers had the key, the committee found a quantity of bacon, hams and two pieces of beef which the matron said was her own private property. On asking to be shown another cellar, the matron told them that the key had been lost for some time and orders were given to force the door open. Inside they found a quantity of wine bottles, both full and empty, and a large supply of candles. Once again Mrs Rogers stated that, with the exception of the candles, they were all her property. The committee informed her that they would have to pass on their findings to the Guardians. During the Board meeting when the matter, and Mrs Rogers part in it, was being discussed, one of the Guardians remembered that reporters were in the meeting. He stated that comments were being made about the character of Mrs Rogers and that he did not think the matter should be discussed further until an enquiry was carried out. This was agreed, and the visiting committee was asked to report to the Guardians the following week.

The matter dragged on for weeks, and by 2 January 1862 Mrs Rogers had obtained the services of a firm of solicitors, Messrs Parker & Sons. The solicitors notified the Guardians that on Mrs Rogers' instructions they had written to the Poor Law Board demanding an enquiry into the matter. In the meantime Mrs Rogers had been advised by her solicitors not to answer any questions on the subject, a development which was making any investigation impossible. On 22 May 1862 there was a report from the visiting committee that, according to the books of the new master, Mr Westcoe, there were deficiencies in the stores. He had done some stocktaking and he had found a deficiency of 67 yards of calico, 61 yards of Forfar sheeting, 304 yards of linsey wool, 160 yards of gingham and 94 yards of Russian towelling. It was found that there were several 'false entries' made in the clothing, material and conversion book which was kept by both the master and matron. It also revealed that the stores had been kept locked but, when things were needed out of the stores, that any of the paupers would be given the key to fetch a required item. As a consequence, during the previous year there were forty or fifty paupers who had access to the stores. More significantly, there was some hostility between the new master and old matron which had caused divisions in the staff. When Mrs Rogers was finally examined at the official enquiry made by the visiting committee in August 1862 she told the Board that following the death of her husband, and whilst she was away ill, she had given the store keys to Mrs Morgan, the assistant matron. Previously she had entered all the material which had been distributed and therefore 'could not hold herself responsible for the missing articles'. The committee agreed that there were several people responsible for the deficiencies, and the conclusions were:

The want of knowledge and firmness on the part of the master
The long continued illness and want of rigid care on the part of the matron
The lax management of the Guardians
The bad feeling existing between the master and matron

All these reasons had caused the opportunities for unauthorised people using the stores and the items going missing. The Guardians expressed an opinion that nearly all concerned in the management of the workhouse in the past year had been to blame, and that 'they can only hope that so great a state of things may never again occur in the Sheffield union workhouse'. It was also agreed that the master would now take the responsibility for the stores; they regretted that the Guardians had not appointed a person to take on the matron's role during her long illness following the death of her husband. In June of 1862 the Guardians received a letter from Mrs Rogers complaining that the cook was in the habit of watering down the hash and the beef tea. She also claimed that some workhouse officers were kept waiting for their dinner. A committee was formed after the work of the Board had finished and discussed the matter for three hours: the only resolution that could be made was that 'the committee deeply regret that the time of the Guardians should be taken up by frivolous matters as the charges just enquired into.'

The investigation revealed that Mrs Rogers was not only antagonistic towards the master but also towards the cook, referring to her as 'that woman'. The chair told the Guardians that he intended to ask Mrs Rogers to resign the following week, due to the factions which she had caused to develop within the workhouse and even within the Board of Guardians itself, some of the Guardians supporting the matron and others for the master. At the following Board meeting, held on 2 July 1862, the chair stated his resolution to ask for Mrs Roger's resignation but did not want to give a reason. Another Guardian, Mr Youdan, said that 'in that case I shall move next week that the master be asked to resign'. Another Guardian, Mr Mills, stated mysteriously that, 'I think there are things happening in this house that need to be brought to light'. It was finally resolved that Mrs Rogers would indeed be asked to resign.

The following week the Guardians received a letter from Mrs Rogers refusing to comply with the resolution demanding her resignation. They sent the letter and the resolution to the Poor Law Board asking them to order her to resign, on account of her 'want of good feeling towards the master, her inattention and neglect of her duties and general obstructive conduct'. The Poor Law Board disagreed and wrote to the Guardians in August stating that 'if Mrs Rogers refuses to resign the Board of Guardians cannot compel her to do so'. One of the Guardians, Mr Crawshaw, felt that the Guardians should demand that an enquiry be held into the matter by the Poor Law Inspector, Mr Mainwaring. The chair objected to this, as he had a strong dislike of any Inspectors coming to the workhouse. 'Don't let,' he asked, 'a little knot of gentlemen in London dictate to them what they should or should not do'.

Mr Crawshaw said that the Guardians must give Mrs Rogers a chance to vindicate herself by means of an investigation. The chair felt that the matter had been fully investigated in great detail by the visiting committee, and that if they had no power to appoint or dismiss officers then the Poor Law Board had better 'undertake the entire management of the union themselves'. It was then put to Mrs Rogers, as an opportunity to recover her character, that another full investigation be undertaken by the Guardians. She declined.

Nevertheless, following yet more allegations about Mrs Rogers and the other officers of the workhouse, another investigation began on Friday 18 October and lasted till Wednesday, 23 October 1862. Accusations were heard from the cook, who said she had been unable to prepare the usual Friday puddings because Mrs Rogers had withdrawn assistants from the kitchen. This had resulted in a note being sent from Mrs Rogers to one of the Guardians, Mr Crawshaw, asking him to 'keep that insolent woman the cook in her place'. There was a charge that she had criticised the opinion of the Medical Officers and had referred to the master as 'that man'. Mr Westcoe stated that he had been master now for a year and that the relationship between them had deteriorated to such an extent that he agreed that one or the other should resign. The Guardians had no option but to suspend her. The chair stated that:

- the Guardians having had their offer of a investigation declined by Mrs Rogers and finding it impossible to conduct the affairs of the house as long as she remains

- that the Poor Law Board at present refuse to assist them in the discharge of their arduous duties unless they consent to be degraded in the eyes of their servants and officers
- that the continuing disagreements and want of cordiality between the master and matron of the workhouse is acting injuriously to the interests of the union and such disagreements being entirely caused in the opinion of this Board by the want of good feeling on the part of the matron towards the master

The Guardians resolved that 'on these grounds and on general neglect of duty, Mrs Rogers be suspended from the discharge of her duties as matron of the workhouse'. The deputy matron, Mrs Ann Pringle, was temporarily appointed in her place until the post could be advertised. A Miss Day was appointed in January 1863. She had been a former assistant matron at Nottingham workhouse, 'having under her control 500 women and children'. She was described in the local newspaper as being 'a young person of superior address.' Thankfully Miss Day proved to be a very valuable asset to the Sheffield workhouse, and the relationship between herself and Mr Westcoe remained good. She had not been in position for very long when she informed the visiting committee that there was not enough clothing in the stores and that almost a third of the paupers had insufficient clothing. So pleased were the Guardians with her behaviour – or perhaps so relieved at finally getting rid of Mrs Rogers – that just eighteen months later her salary was increased from £30 to £50 a year. The reason given for this increase, as one of the Board cheerfully stated, was that 'the matron has discharged her duties to the satisfaction of all the Guardians'.

It appears that some traditional celebrations were enjoyed by the inmates of the Kelham Street workhouse. Mr Westcoe reported a strange 'carry on' over Christmas of 1863. It seems that he had left the workhouse on Christmas Eve for some time. When he returned, about 10.40 p.m., he went to the asylum ward and, entering by a pass key, found the ward assistants, Mr and Mrs Nicks, Nurse Kenney, some hospital women, three inmates from the venereal ward, Mrs Bretnor (described as a woman who waited on the master) and five or six able-bodied men all together. He established that the party had consisted of women with blackened faces kissing officers of the workhouse; some of the able-bodied paupers had been kissing an officer's wife. He also reported singing and Morris dancing going on in the ward. This was probably part of an ancient and traditional Christmas ceremony where 'mummers' would adopt black or red face make-up to disguise themselves, and would visit people in such disguises. On making enquiries he found that several people had heard his footsteps and had already disappeared, including the assistant master, Mr Pringle. Some of these men were found in the nurse's day room the following morning, unable to complete their escape. One of the Guardians, Mr Bassett, tried to say that 'it was just a Christmas lark', but the chair reminded him that if it had been confined to the paupers themselves it could have been viewed with more sympathy. As it was between officers and inmates, it was 'subversive of all discipline'.

A further similar breach of discipline had been heard from Mr Mainwaring the same year. He attended the workhouse on Boxing Day of 1863 and found corridors full of paupers in the process of going out for the day. He spoke to Mr Westcoe, the master, who said that it was tradition to allow the paupers to go into Sheffield on that day and he had merely followed the set precedent. The Inspector requested that the Guardians put a stop to the practice. The chair remarked that it was easier said than done: two of the visiting committee had attended the workhouse on that day and had tried to put a stop to it, but they 'nearly got their heads knocked off'. The paupers pushed them out of the way, hooting and stamping and hissing at them in a most violent manner. Certainly the tradition was still being adhered to by Christmas of 1879. In January of that year, the master told the Guardians that on Boxing Day, of the 140 women who went out, sixty-nine returned late (and of these, eighteen were drunk). Ten never returned at all. The day after Boxing Day, 286 men went out: eighty-nine returned back late, twenty-one were drunk and, once again, sixteen never returned at all. This lack of discipline was put down to the time of year and the fact that beer was issued as a treat for the inmates at Christmas, which naturally made them unruly. The master complained that the worst behaviour was seen amongst the woman; seven or eight had returned to the workhouse so drunk at 10 p.m. that they 'danced an obscene dance at the workhouse door, which was continued as they also were sent into the vagrant ward'.

At a Board meeting on Wednesday, 22 December 1880 it was proposed by the Guardians that instead of the beer which had been given to the inmates the previous year, tea and coffee be served instead. However, the Guardians were lenient: bearing in mind at the time of the offences there had been a total of 1,181 paupers in the house, and that it would

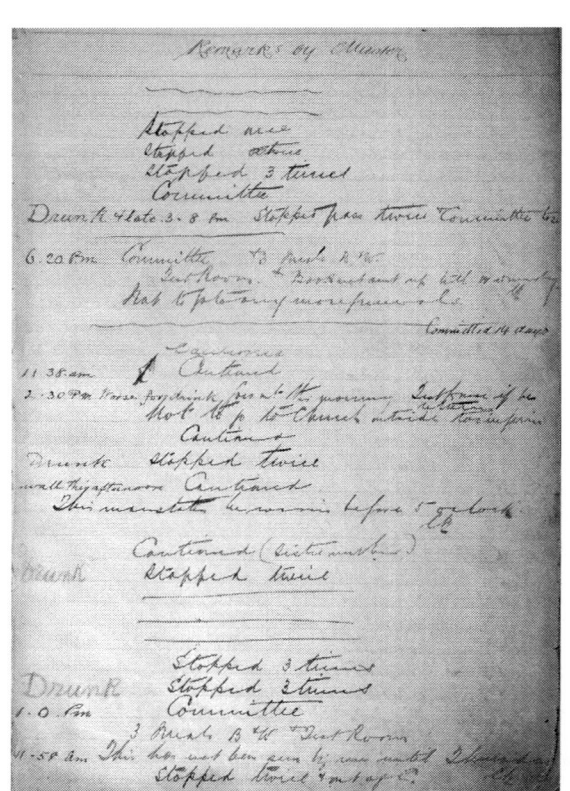

Masters' punishment book, with insertions stating 'drunk' written in red ink.

not be fair to deprive beer to the rest of the house for the transgressions of the few, they decided to continue the beer ration.

The master of any workhouse had to keep a punishment book to present before the Guardians every week. The punishment books for the period of study have been lost, but later ones, dated 1903 to 1926, still exist. Most of the entries were about inmates coming back late to the workhouse after being granted a pass to go to church in the town; in cases where they returned home drunk, the word was inserted in red ink. The passes had to be signed by the minister of the attended church and there were strict repercussions for those who were late back. The recalcitrant inmates who returned back drunk or late were punished by being given a diet of bread and water. On 27 October 1903, John Norton, aged ninety-three, was returned from absconding and was put into the infirm ward for his trouble. Three years later, William Claxby, aged sixty-nine, was cautioned for returning back to the workhouse three quarters of an hour late (he claimed that he had 'got the wrong tram'). On 13 February 1906, William Smith was brought to the workhouse directly from the court house by Attendant Gilman; his punishment was that he was not allowed to have any more passes for a set period of time. A similar complaint was made by one of the workhouse inmates in December 1891: James Malloy complained that the master had not allowed him to see some friends who had come to see him on a visiting order. He appeared before the Guardians, but the master told them that on three previous occasions, when he had been out of the workhouse on a pass, he had stopped out over the expected time that he was allowed, and on one occasion he had been locked up by the police. After a full enquiry the Guardians upheld the decision of the master.

These are some of the masters and matrons of Sheffield workhouse. As we have seen, the Sheffield Guardians were not the easiest people to work with and it could be suggested that this characteristic rubbed off on its officers. The role of master and matron was inevitably one of power over vulnerable inmates – and the most vulnerable of all were the children.

nine

Children in the Workhouse

Despite the concern of the Guardians and the Poor Law authorities about the detrimental effect that the workhouse would have on children, the workhouse was not always a bad place for a child to live. Some children thrived in the workhouse which, grim though it undoubtedly was, was marginally better than living in the streets of the town. On 27 January 1876, an article appeared in the *Sheffield and Rotherham Independent* describing a boy's life in the Kelham Street workhouse. Instead of the image of Oliver Twist, the pauper writing had found 'nothing but solicitous care from the Guardians of the poor within the walls of the old cotton mill'. Indeed his only criticism was the lack of books to read, but he said:

> The union was my cradle, nursery and school and in retrospect of those early day it was not sad but joyous. We were comfortably housed, well clothed and well fed. I well remember the Sunday breakfast which seemed to make the day doubly welcomed and then afterwards we went to church and truly did we enter His gates with thanksgiving. Dinner was more enjoyable under such circumstances and a blessing was sung before and after every meal. I do think that if more books were provided for reading it would be better as we felt the want of books very much. A useful library attached to each union and the educational standards raised is the only improvement that is really needed.

Certainly this unnamed pauper seemed to have enjoyed his time in the Sheffield workhouse. However, the Guardians believed in getting the children out of the workhouse as much as possible and welcomed any kind of invitation which would take them out of the house for a few hours. The children were often invited to attend outings of a religious nature, such as a gathering at Pitsmoor Church in April 1890 or Sunday School Union meetings later the same month. They were also invited to Band of Hope meetings on a regular basis and a gala in June of 1890. Local industries would help out with the arrangements (indicating the philanthropic feeling of Sheffield's businessmen towards the workhouse children). The Guardians expressed thanks on one occasion to Mr George Senior, Mr Chambers of the Midland Railway Co. and Mr Jarvis of the Sheffield Forge

Derwent Hall, which the workhouse children were invited to visit in August 1890.

and Rolling Mill for their kindness in providing horses and drays for the conveyance of the children going to the gala. There was also an invitation from Lady Edmund Talbot in August 1890 for all the workhouse children to visit her home at Derwent Hall. Lady Mary was the wife of Edmund FitzAllen-Howard, the 1st Viscount FitzAllen of Derwent. It is a tribute to her memory that she took time from her duties to entertain the children from the workhouse. Sadly, Derwent Hall no longer exists: it was compulsory purchased in 1939, but was lost when the area was flooded for the Ladybower Reservoir in 1945. In times of drought, however, the Hall makes its appearance once again. The workhouse children would no doubt have been awed by the resplendence of this house as they were conveyed to the Hall in waggonettes. The Guardians' Minutes mentioned that 'on their arrival they were treated in a most generous manner'.

Sadly, a workhouse child died on what should have been a happy occasion on Bank Holiday Monday, 2 June 1879. It seems that 200 of the workhouse children had been invited to the house of the chair of the Guardians, Alderman Searle, at Birkendale for the afternoon. Older workhouse children were able to walk, but twenty-two of the younger ones were taken to the house and back in a horse and cart owned by the Guardians and driven by an inmate, Mr Samuel Sanderson, aged fifty-two. The cart containing the children included a five-year-old child called Florence Denman and a nurse called Ann Dayton. Both Denman and Sanderson died in a tragic accident involving the cart that day, and an inquest was held on Tuesday 3 June at the Infirmary in front of the coroner, Mr D. Wightman. The cause of the accident was established as a broken harness which caused the horse to gallop down the hill. The driver, Sanderson, was thrown out of the cart, and the horse and cart went over his legs. The nurse, Miss Dayton, was also thrown out of the cart, but managed to hold onto the steps as she was dragged down the hill. The master of the workhouse, Mr W.G. Ward, attended the inquest and told the jury that Samuel Sanderson had been at the workhouse for four years, was an experienced carter and had worked with the same horse for most of that time. He told the coroner that the girl's father and a woman thought to be his wife had entered the workhouse with Florence and several other children a few months previously. The woman, unfortunately, had died, and the father was given permission to leave the children in the Fir Vale workhouse in order to seek employment and to 'turn himself around'. But once he left the workhouse he then refused to maintain the children. When he was brought before the magistrates it was proved that he was not married to the children's mother and the case was dismissed, the children remaining in the care of the Guardians. The coroner and the jury questioned Mr Ward about Sanderson and he was asked if the man had been sober at the time of the accident; he replied that he had. He was questioned about the harness, and whether it was new or second-hand. He stated that it was new and had been made by Mr Hobson of Westbar.

A housemaid named Emma Blackhurst, aged twenty-two, was working at the house of Alderman Searle and she gave evidence at the inquest. She told the coroner that she didn't see what happened but heard a scream at about 7 p.m., just as the children were leaving. She ran out of the garden and saw the horse galloping down the hill. She ran after the cart and saw that a man had finally managed to stop the horse at the bottom of the hill – but Florence Denman had been thrown from the cart and was lying in the road. She told the inquest that the little girl was still alive but insensible. One of the men who had witnessed the accident carried her to the Infirmary in his arms, but she died on the way. A jury member commented that twenty-two children in one cart was an excessive amount of weight and it was not surprising that the harness had broken under the strain. The coroner decided that he was not going to ask the jury to make a decision on that day, but would adjourn the inquest to the following Friday. He felt that someone should have been responsible for the number of children in one cart, and he wanted the jury to see the harness for themselves. The inquest was re-opened on Friday 6 June at the Alma Hotel, and the jury returned a verdict of 'accidental death', with a suggestion that more attention be paid to the supervision of the children.

As we have seen, the Guardians were usually happy for the children to go out of the workhouse on different activities, but in January 1880 the Guardians were faced with a dilemma which would drag on for years to come. The problem started when the children were invited to attend a pantomime at the Alexandra Theatre in Sheffield. Opposition to the invitation was not due to the content of the pantomime, but the venue: it was to be held in a theatre, which was seen by some of the Guardians as 'a den of iniquity'. One of the Guardians clearly stated that, 'I wouldn't let my children go to that theatre. It is one of the lowest places in the town and full of the most disreputable types'. He was overruled on this occasion, but the matter would come back to haunt the Guardians year after year.

The following year the matter was discussed once more when they received a letter from Mr Callender, the proprietor for the Lyceum Theatre in Sheffield, inviting the children to attend a pantomime there. One of the Guardians, Mr Joel, objected because there was a bar in the theatre, but he agreed that if the bar was closed he would have no objection. Another Guardian, Mr Barkworth, complained 'that there were no children in the town so indulged as the workhouse children'. He told the Board that he personally would never consent to his own children going to a theatre 'as they were demoralizing places and it was the Guardian's duty to keep the workhouse children away from such influences'. The matter was put to the vote: five voted for and six against, so once again the offer was turned down. The following month another invitation was received from another theatre, and once again the subject was aired. The chair insinuated that the matter was proving irksome as he was aware that when certain Guardians knew that the matter was to be discussed they made sure they attended

The Alexandra Theatre in Sheffield, said to be a 'den of iniquity'.

Lyceum's production of *Aladdin*, which the workhouse children were not allowed to attend.

as a group in order to strongly oppose the offers. The chair pointed out that the Guardian's opposition to the children going to the pantomime had been spoken about in the town, and he felt that local people were critical of their decision. One this occasion the voting was eight for and seven against, so, on this occasion, the children were allowed to attend.

The following February both theatres once again offered to have the children attend their performance, and Mr Carr pointed out that: 'the children should be allowed to go as there was much public feeling in the town from people who felt the children should be allowed to go and that instead of it being a yearly discussion that a definite decision needed to be made'.

He pointed out that the children from the Ecclesall workhouse were allowed to attend the pantomime and that this was unfair on the Sheffield children. On this occasion the voting was even; the chair refused to give a casting vote and so the matter was left in abeyance. During this meeting, a squabble broke out between Mr Joel and Mr Carr, the former claiming 'that [Mr Carr] has told a deliberate lie and if he doesn't withdraw it he is not a gentleman'. It was reported that 'one of the Guardians gave a pacific speech at which the storm was averted' and the chair remarked 'that they were all friends again'. These deliberations regarding attendance at a pantomime seem very trivial to us now. A lot of effort was made by the theatres for these Christmas treats, especially for children. So it does seem unfair that the workhouse children missed out on the opportunity to attend because of the machinations of just a few Guardians.

Children went into the workhouse for many reasons. Some were found begging in the streets and others just appeared on the doorstep. It was reported that a little child, aged about eighteen months, had been left at the entrance lodge of Fir Vale by an unnamed person on 3 January 1880. The Guardians decided that they would give him a name, but typically they couldn't agree on one. It was first decided to call him Richard Searle, after the chair, but another of the Guardians decided that it was more appropriate that the child left at the workhouse should be called Richard Lodge. After some argument, this was finally agreed upon. Two Inspectors of the NSPCC went before the Guardians in July 1890 asking them to take into the workhouse Rose Ann Mackintee as the person who had charge of her had been sentenced to a long term of imprisonment for cruelty. Other children who had been abandoned by parents, and had reached the age where they could go out to work and earn a living, were sometimes snatched back by their parents. It was reported in November 1894 that a girl named Annie Frith, aged fourteen, had been 'enticed' from the workhouse by her mother. The girl was under an Order of Detention and Mr Ashberry and Mr Newsholme were requested to meet with the Chief Constable, Mr Jackson, and 'to take such steps as they think necessary for the girl's recovery', and in this case the girl was recovered safely. When her mother appeared before the Guardians she denied that she had enticed her daughter, who she said had gone of her own accord. However, when Annie told the Guardians that her mother was not married to the man she was living with, the Guardians had no intention of returning the girl back to her mother's care. Instead she was moved to a Catholic Home at Rumford Street, Manchester at a cost of 6s a week; two probable members of the same family, Fred and Ada Frith, were also boarded out to a family at Birchley under the supervision of Father Powell. Other children were not so lucky when they were taken out of the workhouse by a parent. Mrs Towers of Brightside appeared before the Guardians in February 1892 to draw their attention to both her nieces. They had resided in the Fir Vale workhouse until their father had taken them out a fortnight earlier. The girls were Anne Elizabeth and Annie Marie Eyre, aged nineteen and twelve respectively. Their father had arrived and taken the younger girl out of workhouse whilst the elder girl had discharged herself as he said that he had found work for them. They had gone to some lodgings and, after staying with him for one night, he had turned them both out; the distraught aunt told the Guardians that the two girls were at that time living in a pig sty. The Guardians resolved to have the relieving officers make enquiries respecting the youngest girl and ordered that proceedings be taken against the father for desertion.

The Poor Law authorities and the Sheffield Guardians developed many schemes to try to ensure that children could be permanently kept out of the workhouse. One scheme, which had been in place since the earliest years of the workhouse, had been in apprenticing children to various skilled tradesmen in the town. The intention was that they would learn a trade and not become recipients of relief in the future. The small payment which was given to the tradesman as a bonus for taking the child was criticised by opponents of the scheme: it was said that having got a child as a method of cheap labour the tradesman would work the child harder as a consequence. One of the earliest mentions of children being apprenticed out was in 1570; nearly a century later, in 1668, it was recorded in the Town Trustees accounts that 12s was paid to two overseers, John Bayes and Richard Paramour, for two children apprenticed with William Mason. Sometimes children appeared before the Guardians asking for help to get a job. Such a case was heard on 27 January 1870 from a boy who had been in the workhouse for two or three years and who had been described as an orphan. He told the Guardians that he was in the workhouse with his brother and admitted that he was lame in one leg, which he saw as a disadvantage when seeking a job. He asked them to buy him a horse and cart from which he could sell vegetables. The chair told the Board that he had spoken to the master, who had told him that the boy was a 'good lad' who could read and write. The chair asked all the Guardians to look out for a post for the boy and to instruct the relieving officers to do the same. Whether the lad found a job or not is not recorded, but it seems there is no doubt that the Guardians were sincere in helping him to find something.

On 7 May 1851, the master, Mr Rogers, had been sent to visit all the workhouse children who had gone as apprentices and to report back to the Guardians, and his report was entered in the letter book. He told them that the only complaint from the children was that they didn't have any books of their own. He suggested that when the children go out as apprentices that they be given a Bible to take with them. All girls who were apprenticed were usually sent into domestic service and were given a suitable outfit of clothes if they remained in service.

However much the Guardians agreed with the need for children to be apprenticed, the treatment of some of these children caused discussion in the Boardroom. There was laughter in the room on 7 September 1881 when the Guardians were investigating a claim of a girl who had been taken into service at a cook shop on the Wicker. It seems that she had been fed solely on black puddings and polony (a sausage of smoked meat) and as a result she had been afflicted with scurvy. Despite the laughter, the matter was serious enough for the clerk to be instructed to write to the shop owner and demand that he attend the Guardians and explain the reasons for this strange diet. Some apprentice schemes ended in cruelty to the child. In November 1859, the Guardians were horrified to learn about the ill treatment of a girl who had been sent out as an apprentice nurse to a family in Sheffield. The girl's name was Mary Ann Hogg and the Guardians were informed that she had been taken to the Infirmary following a beating she had received from her employer. The Guardians demanded that the woman be brought to the Boardroom and the following week she appeared. The woman, Mrs Cox, told the Guardians that the girl had 'fallen down the cellar steps'. The girl, who had by now recovered from her injuries, was brought into the Boardroom. She was described as 'being pale and thin and aged about 10 or 12 years of age'. She told the Guardians that on the evening of 12 November her employer, Mrs Cox, had told her to get up at five the following morning and to thoroughly clean the kitchen. She had got up at five, but she was unable to light the fire in order to boil some water as the wood had been damp. When Mrs Cox got up at six and found the kitchen had not been cleaned, she flew into a temper and hit her over the head with a coal rake. In response to a question from one of the Guardians, the girl denied that she had ever fallen down the cellar stairs as Mrs Cox had stated. Mrs Cox was brought back into the room. When she was told what the girl had said, she apologised to the Guardians. The chair pointed out that the girl had been employed as a nurse and that she should not have been doing housework at all. The woman was dismissed and the Guardians decided that the girl should remain at Fir Vale workhouse until another position could be found for her.

Another case of cruelty and abuse was brought before the Guardians in June 1861 to do with a girl aged thirteen years who had been taken out of the Kelham Street workhouse two years previously by a woman called Conyers. She was the wife of Thomas Conyers and lived in Sheldon Street, Sheffield. Mrs Conyers had told the Guardians that she was a boot binder by trade and had apprenticed the girl to teach her the trade. Neighbours complained to the relieving officer that the girl was 'in a dirty state and wore ragged clothes'. They also told him that it was common knowledge that the girl had been forced to sleep with the husband whilst Mrs Conyers slept in the spare room. The relieving officer was appalled and immediately went to see Mr and Mrs Conyers. When he arrived he was told that the girl was out but he spoke to Mrs Conyers, who was aged about forty, and her husband, aged sixty, who both denied all the allegations. On leaving the house he spotted the girl (who he recognised due to the condition of her clothing). She told him that she had better clothes which had been sent to her by an aunt but she had been forced to pawn them by Mrs Conyers. The relieving officer went back to the house and confronted the pair. Mrs Conyers blustered at first but then admitted all the charges. She asked him, 'what happens now?' The relieving officer told her that it would be up to the Guardians and he brought the girl back to the workhouse. When he reported to the Guardians at the next Board meeting, he stated that the girl's mother was dead and her father had deserted her and her sister years ago and therefore the Sheffield Guardians were her only protectors. The girl was brought before the Board and she told them that she lived in fear of Mrs Conyers, who had a bad temper and had recently blacked her eye. She admitted that she had been forced to sleep with the old man for twelve months but swore that no impropriety had taken place. However, the Guardians didn't feel that the girl was telling the truth – they suspected that she been told to say that if anyone asked. Once again, the Guardians agreed that she could stay at the workhouse until another situation could be found for her. After the girl had left the room there was some discussion regarding her treatment but eventually the Board agreed that, legally speaking, there was very little they could do. However, the relieving officer told them that when he spoke to the neighbours they were very incensed at the treatment handed out to her by the couple and that he 'wouldn't be surprised if they went to the house and tore the woman to pieces'.

Despite these atrocious cases, the Guardians saw themselves as protectors of the workhouse children and did their utmost to ensure that the position in which they found themselves was a safe one. In January of 1892 it was agreed by the Guardians that all applications to take girls and boys out of the workhouse as apprentices 'shall be forwarded to the Board from the master'. These requests were to be accompanied by a medical certificate as to the children's health and 'general fitness for the work required of them'. But it was an organisation called the House of Help for Friendless Girls, which took on the roles of supervising these girls in their domestic placements, which finally brought such abuses to an end in August 1889. The women who worked at the House of Help undertook to visit the girls on a regular basis at their place of employment to make sure that they were comfortable and well looked after. If the girls were not working to the required standard, or if any instances of bad behaviour were observed, they would remove

	li.	s.	d.
And with Interrest received of Jonathan Brough-			
ton for 20 li. - - - - - -	1	4	0
And with interrest received of John Styring for			
10 li. - - - - - - - -	0	12	0
Received Jarvis Cooper which he had upon bond	20	0	0
and with a yeares interrest for the same - -	1	4	0
And of John Nodder for interrest af 100 li. for a			
year - - - - - - -	6	0	0
And of Thomas Lemons for interrest of 20 li. -	1	4	0
And of Robert Breilsforth for interrest of 30 li. -	1	16	0
And of Thomas Skargill for interrest of 130 li. -	7	16	0

And with money received of John Bayes[1] and
Richard Parramour[2] overseers of the poore for
the use of 2 children apprentices with William
Mason which is yearly to be paid by the overseers of the poore to the towne collector to be
kept for the use of the said children till they
come att age in lieu of certain houseing[3] belonging to the said children and employed by the

overseers - - - - - . -	0	12	0

Summe totall of the Charge is 188 2 5

Discharge.   Arrears to be respited.

Payment for apprenticeship for two boys with William Mason in 1668.

SHEFFIELD UNION WORKHOUSE.

Regulations in the Sheffield Union Workhouse under which Girls may be taken out for Service.

To be read at the Workhouse to all applicants, by the Master or his Assistant, before they are permitted to select one.

All Girls sent out to service are placed under supervision and control of the Ladies' Committee of the House of Help, who, if they deem it necessary, have authority to remove them.

An outfit of suitable clothing, to the value of £2, is granted to each child that remains in her situation.

Regulations for girl apprentice's with clothing.

This clothing will be furnished through the Ladies' Committee, partly when the girl is first sent out, and the remainder after the expiration of one month, if the Ladies are satisfied.

The Guardians require that wages shall be paid to girls taken out, as may be arranged with the Ladies' Committee, according to the service which the girl is capable of rendering ; but the lowest scale shall be as follows :—

For the three months next following the first month, 6d. per week.

For the three months next following, at the rate of 1s. per week.

For the three months next following, at the rate of 1/6 per week.

The Ladies' Committee will see to the proper expenditure of the girl's earnings, and that they use them to provide themselves with all necessary clothing, so that employers are not required of necessity to incur any further expense in regard to the same.

In the possible event of any misconduct on the part of the girl, the Ladies' Committee or the Matron of the House of Help must be communicated with, and not the Relieving Officer

In no case must the girl be returned to the Workhouse, but should necessity arise she must be taken to the House of Help.

Recommended scale of wages for girls in service from House of Help.

the girls. The workhouse master was instructed to see to the following regulations under which workhouse girls were employed and to ensure that a copy was given to potential employers before they selected an appropriate girl. The regulations also gave guidelines as to the kind of wages which the girl should receive. The House of Help was instrumental in supervising the workhouse girls sent into service and the Guardians acknowledged their help in the Minutes of a meeting held in June 1892 when they noted:

> The Guardians have been for the past three years in receipt of very considerable assistance from the House of Help for Friendless Girls in supervising the material and moral welfare of girls sent into service from the Fir Vale workhouse. This involved frequently placing some of the girls who showed dishonest or immoral proclivities in Reform Homes and Training Institutions which were of great benefit to the girls.

In August of 1894 it was agreed that 'no workhouse girl will be taken into domestic service unless the application came from the House of Help itself'. They also made themselves responsible for looking into the potential employers to make sure that they were respectable. In April of 1895 a report was received by the Guardians listing the girls at that time that had gone out to domestic service. They were:

> Elizabeth Lister: in her second situation and still doing well.
> Florence Rowe: at present at the House of Help having left her first situation. At the end of her second week the committee hopes to send her to a situation in the country shortly.
> Mary Ellen Murray: Father Burke reports well of this girl who is living in his house as an under servant. [On 3 May the girl 'was removed by friends' and Father Burke requested another named child from the workhouse, but she was deemed to be too young, at just twelve, to go into his service.]
> Rebekah Pemberton: has given much trouble but admission has been obtained for her to a Catholic Home for Girls for one year's training to which she went on 26 March.
> Sarah Hooper: has given a good deal of trouble but it is hoped a more favourable report may be presented next month.

In February 1897 a further report was made on Florence Rowe, who was then aged seventeen years. It seems that initially she had gone into a situation where she had remained for over twelve months, but after leaving had 'not been going on at all satisfactory'. It was reported that instead of finding her a situation in the country, she had been for several weeks at the House of Help where the superintendent, Mrs Flather, was having a lot of trouble with her. She suggested to the Guardians that the girl be sent to a home at Wensley Fold in Blackburn, Lancashire, at the expense of 3s 3d a week, which was agreed. The same month it was reported that another Sheffield workhouse girl called Alice Turner had absconded from the position found for her. Mrs Flather reported that she was at a home belonging to the Society for the Rescue of Young Women in London, and a request was made that she be allowed to remain there for another three months. This Society rescued young girls from vice and the crime of prostitution, a situation often entered into by desperate young women with nowhere to go.

Sometimes the Guardians heard about more successful apprenticeships. In November 1894 a girl listed as Mary Ellen Smith, who had been described as 'feeble minded', was removed to the sadly named Home for Feeble Minded Girls at Knowle near Birmingham at a cost to the Guardians of 5s a week. This home taught girls like Mary Ellen a trade which was capable of being done by someone with learning difficulties. Her case was supervised by the Ladies Committee of the House of Help, who reported back to the Guardians that she had been visited in May 1896. At that time she had been working in a laundry for the Homes of Industry where the Ladies Committee had been much impressed by the girl's improvement. Mrs Flather told the Guardians that when the girl finished her training 'in about six month's time', she would be able to earn her own living and support herself.

In September 1896 the House of Help was superceded by another organisation. It had been noted in the Minutes that there had been 'some difficulties' in their relationship in recent weeks although these difficulties were not explained. On 10 September the Guardians agreed the following resolution:

The Guardians tender to the committee of the House of Help our best thanks for the kind and efficient manner in which they have 'mothered' the girls from the Sheffield workhouse who have entered into domestic service and inform them that the Guardians are now transferring the cases of these girls for the future to the New Servants Home. They would like it to be understood that this transfer is desired not because the House of Help committee have in any way failed in their 'mothering' of our girls but because the Servants Home appears to be the most suited to the needs of a respectable domestic servant.

The Guardians also requested the Servant's Home on Upper Gell Street 'be required to take over the powers and duties hitherto performed on behalf of our girls by the House of Help'. However, it does appear that the split had been amicable, as Mrs Flather wrote to the Guardians in November of the same year saying that she had heard that a sub-committee from the Servant's Home was regularly visiting the children's homes. She was pleased that the visits were to be of a friendly and unofficial nature to win the confidence of the foster mothers and the children. These visits would allow the committee to learn the character and capacity of the girls desiring to go into domestic service. She ended that she had great pleasure in expressing her approval of the scheme.

Where girls were apprenticed to situations of domestic service, boys were generally apprenticed to local trades such as cutlers and steel workshops and many others were apprenticed to colliers. A very interesting list of fifty-nine boys who had been apprenticed out since 1879 is to be seen in the Sheffield Guardians' Minutes for 1894/95, a boon for family historians. The report, which was written by Alfred Richards, a superintendent, gives the names and families the boys were apprenticed to, as well as a short history of the children since their apprenticeship. Many were apprenticed to colliers with indentures lasting for seven years. Others were now married with children of their own and some had taken the name of their apprenticed masters. The majority of the boys had done well and were still in work, but many were listed as having absconded. Some of the more detrimental remarks included 'said to be a gambler', 'twice before the bench', 'curses, drinks and swears', 'not fond of work' and 'was saucy and lazy'. Out of the fifty-nine apprentices, thirty-one were working as colliers at that time. Mr Richards makes the suggestion that to stop boys from absconding:

> A small sum of money from the start of the indentures be put into the Post Office or a Savings Bank in the joint names of the master and the apprentice on a regular basis. If the boy absconds the money is repaid to the master and when he finishes his apprenticeships the money is his.

It is well known that coal mines were dangerous places to work, and it was with great sadness the Guardians were informed in August of 1884 that John Ennis, aged fifteen, who had been apprenticed to William Cheetham of Woodhouse in 1879, had been killed in the Fence Colliery Disaster four days previously. One of the receiving officers, Mr Richards, had represented the Guardians by attending the inquest, where a verdict of accidental death had been returned.

Other schemes which the Guardians cheerfully adopted to get children out of the workhouse were the many emigration schemes which were prevalent at the end of the 1800s. These schemes, such as the Catholic Church Children's Protection Society or the Canadian Emigration and Employment Bureau, found homes and employment for children who expressed a wish to go to Canada. Mr and Mrs W.J. Pady contacted the Guardians of the local workhouses and gathered together groups of children who had agreed to join the scheme and escorted them on their voyage. This seems very strange to our more modern minds, as the scheme must have been open to all kinds of abuse to the children landing in a strange new land. What is more difficult to understand is that the same Guardians that had argued long and hard about sending children to watch a pantomime would cheerfully send them thousands of miles away, alone and friendless. The Guardians regularly received glowing reports about the successful emigration of children to Canada in 1888 and '89. The Local Government Board wrote to the Guardians to inform them that they had also received reports on nine children who had been sent to Canada under this scheme in 1891, which said to be 'very satisfactory'.

Many of these emigration schemes were criticised for lack of supervision of the children whilst travelling and lack of the checks made on potential adoptive parents. The reality was that many of these parents wanted children to work and even small children were expected to share in household duties. Nevertheless, the Guardians had nothing but positive reports for the children that had been sent to Canada. In 1894 it was reported that some of the children had been visited by a Mr Smith of Toronto, who was an agent for the Hamilton Government Emigration Office. He was employed by the Canadian government to visit all the emigrant children to ensure their well being. He informed the Sheffield Guardians that the children were happy and settled and that 'the Guardians might safely place their children in the Canadian homes allotted to them'. By June 1894 there were twenty-three names of children who had been orphaned or deserted at Fir Vale workhouse agreeing to go to Canada. We have no evidence whether or not these children really were orphans or how carefully the relieving officers endeavoured to find any relatives in this country before agreeing to allow them to go. The Guardians were no doubt delighted at the prospect of giving these children a new life in a healthier environment. But we have to conclude that the separation of these children from any remaining relatives must have had a massive effect on them. In Lynn Howsam's excellent *Memories of Life in the Workhouse and the Old Hospital at Fir Vale* there is an account of a young man who was sent out to Canada under one of these schemes in April 1910. He was Harold Dodham, and his experiences were very different from the ones reported above. Rather than the Guardians, he had been sent to Canada under the auspices of the Dr Barnado's scheme. He talks about his feelings of bewilderment at arriving at Quebec as the children were rounded up in a cattle yard with no idea where they were going to be sent. Sisters and brothers were separated with no consultation. He stated that he was left sitting in a train with slat seating, alone, with a label around his neck marked with his destination, Tully Farm, Perth. The farms where the children were sent were generally small and isolated and they needed workers. The British children – due no doubt to many years of privation – could not compare to the better-fed Canadian children who, despite their size, were worked from dawn to 9 p.m.

A very different scheme for getting children out of the workhouse had a rather mixed reception from the Sheffield Guardians when it was introduced by the Poor Law Board in November 1870. The Boarding-Out scheme was described to the Guardians as one where workhouse children went to live with working-class families, very like the fostering families we are familiar with today. Small payments were made to these families to cover the costs of food and clothing, and the children were expected to be treated as members of the family. The children would have access to Medical Officers for any health issues and the relieving officers were given the task of visiting the families from time to time to make sure the children were well cared for. In Sheffield, when an application was received, enquiries were made into the foster carer's character. Providing they were acceptable, they were then requested to attend the workhouse and 'select a suitable child'. This seems a rather barbaric process, which once again must have been open to many abuses. One of the Guardians, Mr Wood, totally supported the scheme, stating that once the children were introduced into respectable homes they would merge into society like other children, learn to work and never trouble the Guardians again. But many of his colleagues did not agree and despite the success of the scheme in other places the Guardians were opposed to it for the Sheffield workhouse children. The chair pointed out that they would have to pay the adoptive parents 4s a week for each child, besides providing it with school fees and clothing. However, his main concern was not the cost of the scheme but the inability of workhouse children to change, stating that 'even in the best of families the Guardians would not be altering their blood and bones'. He was reprimanded for this remark by another Guardian, Mr Turnell, who said, 'I am sorry to hear you make that observation as these children are human beings'. The chair answered him, 'you could take them to the skies and you could not alter their nature. Many of them seem naturally lazy and nothing will alter them.'

In the end, due to the very serious nature of the question, it was decided to adjourn the debate for a fortnight. When the matter was returned to there was even more opposition to the scheme. Mr Shipman stated that he felt the system would fail due to three reasons: that the Boarded out children would not receive proper parental care; that the respectable working people of Sheffield would not receive a workhouse child into their homes; and that as a consequence of the premium paid to parents, 'the children would be brought up by the lowest classes and therefore be subject to their evil influences'.

Alderman Saunders stated that as the children were already kept separate from the workhouse inmates at the school at Pitsmoor there was no need for them to be boarded out. They were free from the bad influences of the workhouse, and when they were old enough to go to work they were given good apprenticeships where persons were always willing to take them on. The rest of the Guardians agreed and there were shouts of 'hear hear'. Mr Turnell once again tried to persuade his colleagues that the Local Government Board did not mean that the Guardians would lose sight of the children who were boarded out; in fact, they would be visited regularly. He asked that some of the children be boarded out as a trial, but the chair, who had clearly stated his position, reminded his colleagues that children boarded out would cost the ratepayer 4s a week and keeping them in the workhouse would cost 2s 9d. Mr Robertshaw also opposed the scheme, saying that the selection of children for boarding out would be like a slave market and the parents selecting a child would choose the one likely to eat the least. The Guardians took a vote on the issue and that matter was abandoned.

However, eventually the Sheffield Guardians took on (or were forced to take on) the scheme. The Minutes record that in April of 1890 an application had been received from Mr John Earnsworth of Fukes Cottage to have a boy boarded out to him. It was agreed that his case was suitable and that he could select a child, and he chose a young man called George William Colton. It may be that the children were boarded out on trial, as the records indicate that Mr Earnsworth was to be allowed £2 a year for clothing and 3s 6d a week for thirteen weeks. Another request was heard from Mr Thomas Teather of 89 Brompton Road who requested a boarded out girl and he too was invited to select a suitable candidate, but there is no further mention of her in the Minutes. In May 1890 the uncle of a boy named Wilkinson made an application in person to the Guardians to take his nephew from the workhouse. He wanted to have him adopted by a Mr Pochin of Ranmoor who had expressed a willingness to adopt and take him to his house to bring him up as 'a page'. He was informed that he must apply in the usual way. The boarding out scheme now continued with much success and several children were found homes in Birchley under the auspices of the Birchley Boarding Out Committee. They informed the Guardians in November 1894 that, as three of the children were now leaving to find employment at fourteen years of age, they would be prepared to find homes for one or two other children. Two eligible children were selected, both aged twelve years. They were Margaret Martin and John Thomas Quinn. However, although no explanation is given, it seems that on 9 May 1895 an application was put before the Guardians for medical expenses and funeral costs for the little girl, Margaret Martin.

But despite the initial hostility of the Guardians to the boarding out scheme, it paved the way for a further scheme that was embraced with much success by the Sheffield Guardians. The scheme was taken up with much enthusiasm and was called the Scattered Homes scheme.

ten

Scattered Homes

What was to prove the Sheffield Guardian's greatest success started very innocuously in December of 1890, when the Local Government Board authorised the Sheffield Guardians to form a committee to find and supervise a 'Home for Deserted and Abandoned Pauper Children'. In May of 1891 it was brought to the Guardian's attention that a parcel of land from a nearby estate was coming onto the market. The chair informed them of the auction to sell off the house and land known as Goddard Hall. Mr Kennedy, the Local Government Board Inspector, was present at the meeting and he readily agreed to the sale. The auctioneers were actually selling off three plots of land in one piece, bought by the chair for the sum of £4,000. The plots of land were quite substantial and included land, the building known as Goddard Hall, plus a cottage, stable, coach house and outbuildings (as well other land adjoining the Fir Vale workhouse itself). The Guardians were unsure how it would be used, and in the interim period, July of 1891, the workhouse master was instructed to send two inmates, preferably a man and wife, to live in Goddard Hall and to act as caretakers.

By June of 1891 it had been established that there were thirty-seven children in the workhouse classified as being destitute and without parents. Mr John Wycliffe Wilson, the chair of the Guardians, took a great interest in the workhouse children; he was a great supporter of the Cottage or Scattered Home Scheme as being the most suitable system for the poor children of Sheffield. These were small homes which would hold about fifteen to twenty children, who would be taken care of by appointed foster parents. Mr Wycliffe Wilson became Lord Mayor of Sheffield in 1902 and his generosity to the workhouse children resulted in them spending afternoons at his house, where he regularly invited them to tea. More than likely he would have been part of a deputation to visit West Derby Cottage Homes on Thursday, 29 September 1892. The Local Government Board, although they approved of the scheme, were very much against the principle of scattered homes throughout the town, preferring for the children's homes to stay together in one area. In July 1891 the clerk read out a letter from Mr Kennedy, who stated that:

Goddard Hall.

with reference to the disposal of workhouse children the Local Government Board are of the opinion that any proposal for setting up Scattered Homes dotted about various areas on the outskirts of Sheffield would not be assented to, but there would be no difficulties raised about providing a suitable site for Cottage Homes for the children but they must be near to each other.

Originally the Guardians agreed. They decided that the headquarters of the scheme would be Goddard Hall itself, where three homes would be built on the land surrounding the Hall. In February 1894, the Local Government Board authorised £16,744 for the erection of the three Cottage Homes, a children's hospital and other buildings on the site. But before the estate could be built suitable houses would be rented to accommodate the workhouse and their foster parents throughout Sheffield. It is more than likely that the success of the homes being in different places throughout the town brought home to the Guardians the suitability of the scheme. The Sheffield Guardians decided that the Scattered Home approach had worked and removed from the children completely the stigma of the workhouse. It was agreed that suitable houses which could be turned into homes for the children were to be advertised for in June 1893. As was usual, a special committee was set up to organise this. The members of the committee went out to inspect the various houses and reported back to the Guardians on their findings. It was decided that, as the scheme was experimental, the houses would originally be rented for a year before any decision could be made to buy the properties. On 2 June 1893 they reported that they had examined houses suitable for the scheme whose annual rental was between £25 and £50 a year. By September they had appointed eight foster mothers, all married women, who were to be paid £18 a year, and it was agreed that they were allowed one half day a week off. Mrs Lucy Stocks was appointed as the supernumery foster carer, to take over the duties of the foster mothers in cases of sickness (or on the days off) at the same salary.

The appointed houses were to be furnished and made ready for use as soon as possible. Medical officers of health were appointed, whose duties were to visit the children monthly and as often as necessary in the case of sickness. He was to supply all medicines and submit a report to the Guardians every quarter, and for this extra work he would be given 2s 6d for each child. It was also part of his duties to give advice and medicine to the foster parents as required. The workhouse schoolmaster, Mr Nicks, who now had no pupils at the school, was appointed as superintendent to the Scattered Homes and instructed to visit daily and find out what stores were needed. He also had to be responsible under the Guardians for the proper conduct and discipline of the homes and their inmates. The Ladies' Visiting Committee were appointed to visit the homes every week and a visitor's book was to be kept for every home. As with other workhouse officers, the books were to be presented before the Guardians at their weekly meetings. Some of the homes were provided for Catholic children and others allocated for Protestant children, and churches were allocated to each home.

The regulations were very clear. They were:

- Two children aged over seven years will not be allowed to share the same bed.
- No boys over seven years can share the same dormitory as girls.
- Boys over thirteen years are not to be placed in the same home as girls except in the case of brother and sister.

Although the original intention was for deserted and orphaned children to be in these homes by September 1893, other workhouse children were placed there instead. Finally, the Guardians had a scheme which would successfully remove all children from the Fir Vale workhouse. It had been agreed that visiting time for these children would be kept to a strict timetable. Parents who were in the workhouse would be given a pass and allowed to visit on the third Saturday of the month. It was not long before this rule was broken, and the foster mothers began to complain about parents turning up at other times. In January 1894 the master brought it to the Guardian's attention that, of twenty-two parents who had applied for a pass to visit their children in the Cottage Homes, only two parents had returned to the workhouse at the proper time. Two others had not returned at all. The matter was reported to the Cottage Homes' committee. Once again, in August of 1894, it was reported that the parents of children in the homes were visiting at irregular hours and insisting on seeing their children. The superintendent was asked to submit the parents' names and addresses to the committee; they would then undertake to visit each parent to ensure that they only visited at the appointed time. Once the headquarters, formerly Goddard Hall, had been opened in December 1894 the parents still residing in the workhouse were instructed that they had to meet their children there at the appointed hour. A barber was

John Wycliffe Wilson, a supporter of the Scattered Homes scheme.

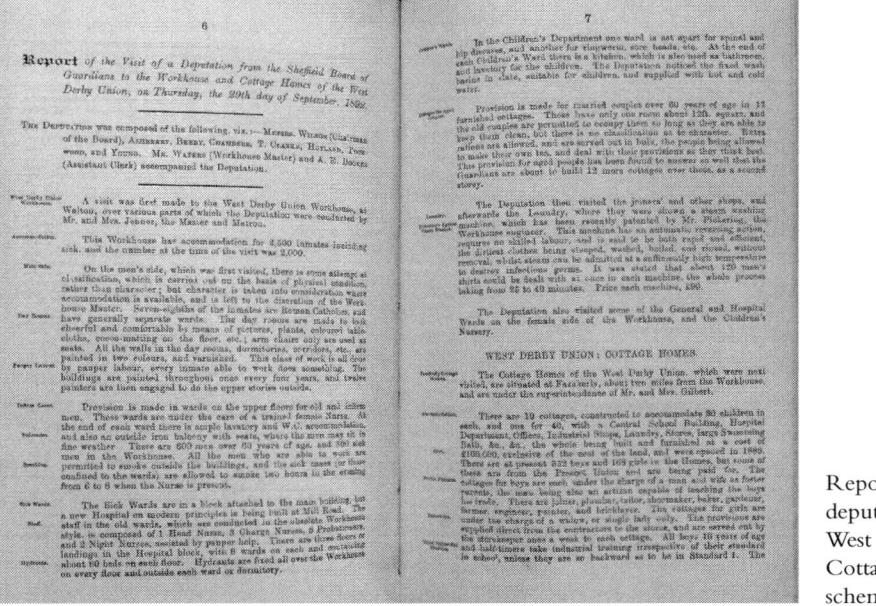

Report of deputation to West Derby Cottage Homes scheme.

appointed for the children at a salary of £4 10s a year and a dentist, Mr W.B. Tolputt, was appointed in July 1895 at a salary of £25 p.a. Mr Tolputt soon noticed that the children had to share toothbrushes and he requested that individual toothbrushes be supplied to all the younger children; a drill of teeth brushing was to take place every night. Books were collected as a library to be kept at the headquarters for the children. Boxes were made for each child to keep under their beds to store their clothing and any belongings. You can almost sense the excitement of the Guardians as their plans for the Cottage Homes begin to unfold. It was decided in May 1894 that the scheme would be called Sheffield Children's Homes (rather than 'Cottage Homes' as formerly). However, in the press they continued to be referred to as the Scattered Homes Scheme.

The Goddard Hall headquarters was opened with great ceremony by Sir Walter Foster, MP, the Parliamentary Secretary to the Local Government Board, on Saturday, 24 November 1894. He spoke of the scheme:

> …having the approval of all well-thinking citizens, and everyone would be delighted with the completion of the scheme which has occupied the Sheffield Board of Guardians for the last three years. The scheme is still very much an experiment and the removal of the children from the contamination of workhouse life has been a problem with which the Guardians have been engaged in with much success. Barrack schemes have been started in Birmingham, Manchester and Liverpool but the Sheffield Guardians favoured small Cottage Homes in various suburbs each to contain not more than 15 children. The little folk will be brought up by foster parents and in surroundings as nearly as possible assimilating to those of average artisans' children.

He praised Mr John Wycliffe Wilson as the prime mover of the scheme and praised his enthusiasm and energy, which had driven the scheme forward, stating that 'it was a pleasure for him to see the realisation of their hopes'. The gates in the wall surrounding the headquarters were opened with due ceremony and the party entered to inspect the buildings. Through the gates was the lodge which held the administrative section and the receiving wards for about twenty children and their parents. The wards include a Medical Officer's room, examination rooms with a bath and a waiting room for foster parents. The superintendent's quarters commanded a view of the road and the main buildings. The three detached homes where some of the children were to live were to be named Ivy Cottage, Rose Cottage and Hawthorne Cottage, and were situated to the west of the entrance, each having a piece of garden, a playground and a wash house. Electric bells were fitted throughout and it was reported that 'great care has been given to the layout of the buildings which had been designed by the architect Mr C.J. Innocent of George Street, Sheffield'. It was agreed that a separate children's hospital would be opened within the site. Such was the success of the scheme that a deputation came from Mansfield union workhouse to Sheffield on Friday, 12 November 1894 to inspect the houses. Once the official opening had taken place, the buildings were thrown open to the public for inspection on Thursday, 6 December 1894, from 2 p.m. to 5 p.m. The following month it was recorded that there were sixty-eight boys and fifty-seven girls in the scattered houses around Sheffield, and fifty-one boys and fifty-six girls in the headquarters' cottages.

At this time, once again, the Guardians were having trouble with their officers: there were some unnamed allegations made about the conduct of two of the foster carers in April of 1895. The committee had been asked to look into the complaints regarding Mrs Lucy Stocks, who had been appointed as one of the relief mothers, and Mrs Osbourne.

Ivy Cottage at the headquarters.

When the committee reported back it was resolved that the Guardians ask for both women's resignation. Although there is no record of what Mrs Stocks' misdemeanours were, the Guardians were of the opinion that:

> Although they regret the resignation of Mrs Stocks it is better taking into account all the other things into consideration.
>
> That Mrs Osbourne in receiving male visitors to the house has not manifested the conduct that became her as a woman having her husband living and they recommend that she be requested to resign.

Both resignations were received on 5 May 1895, but it was not long before more complaints were made against another foster mother named Mrs Hunt. Once again the allegations against her were not outlined, but they may have had something to do with a boy, William Southern, aged six, who received what was described as 'a severe beating by three of the boys of Rose Cottage'. The committee expressed their regret at the occurrence and proposed to administer a severe reprimand to Mrs Hunt 'as soon as her health permits'. The committee stated that it had adopted this course rather then ask for her dismissal 'due to the serious condition of her health and the strong belief that but for her illness her conduct would have been different'. The committee also drew the attention to the fact that foster carers were forbidden to inflict corporal punishment, but it was also agreed that 'they had to prevent chastisement or ill-usage of one child against another'. The committee was also asked in July 1896 to make enquiries and to keep an eye on the home run by Mrs Letts 'over the next fortnight'. She had one of the cottages at the headquarters and they were asked to 'look into the manner in which this mother performs her duties'. A fortnight later, having spoken to Mrs Letts about the condition of the home, they were able to report that there had been a big improvement, and the matter was left to stand for the time being.

Two months later the Guardians were informing the Local Government Board that the children's homes were now fully occupied and that more houses were needed. At that moment in time they had homes at Nos 2 and 4 Oxford Street; 149 and 151 Upperthorpe; Montgomery Terrace Road; 11 and 13 Milner Road, Hillsborough; Burngreave Road; 432 and 434 Grimesthorpe Road; 100 Nottingham Street; 88 and 90 Andover Street.

The Guardians were instructed to advertise for more suitable houses which could be used as children's homes in August 1895. As we have seen, it was the Guardian's intention to ensure that the homes were scattered throughout the districts of Sheffield. They particularly wanted houses in such areas as Pitsmoor, Grimesthorpe, Lower Walkley, Hillsborough, Wadsley Bridge or Southey Green. A plan of the type of rooms for these homes is reprinted opposite. The Local Government Board had stated that the rentals of these houses should be taken out for a year and questioned why the houses on Grimesthorpe Road had been taken out for three years. The Guardians replied that, due to the difficulty in getting suitable property, they felt that the scheme had now gone past the experimental stage, and it was the intention in the future to buy suitable houses at comparatively little risk.

The scheme had been, and continued to be, very successful – although, like any scheme, it had its fair share of problems. In October 1895 the Guardians received a deputation from the Ancient Order of Foresters Friendly Society, who owned six properties at the other side of the street from the children's home on Milner Street. They explained to the Guardians that the investment in the houses was being threatened by the bad behaviour and noise coming from the house. They informed the Guardians that their tenants were threatening to leave if the noise was not abated. They pointed out that it was a serious matter for their Society to have the value of their properties depreciated in this manner. The Guardians asked the superintendent to investigate and report back. In August of 1895, at the second annual meeting, the visiting committee reported to the Guardians that the experiment had been a great success. Now the Sheffield Guardians could confidently state that no child over three years of age would be in the Fir Vale workhouse. The chair added:

> In conclusion we are able to state our unabated confidence in our system of Isolated Children's Homes and we congratulate the Sheffield Board of Guardians and our fellow townspeople that Sheffield has been the first to take this long step in the right direction. Members of other Boards of Guardians continue to visit our Homes and now that the Poor Law Schools Committee have reported so favourably of them, and that the Local Government Board appear to be prepared to sanction our system, something very like it will shortly be widely extended.

The superintendent, Mr Offen, also added his report, declaring that the conduct of the children had been 'very good', and that 'the older girls have attended lectures in laundry

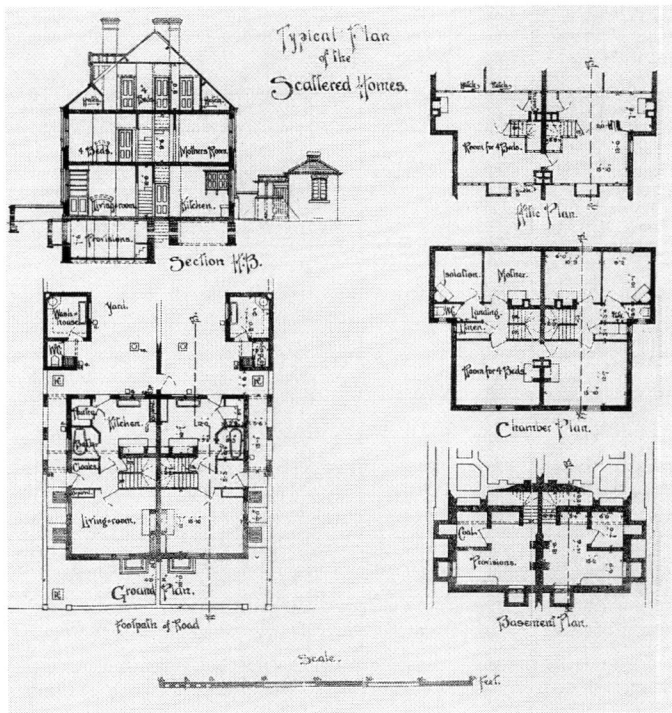

Typical plan for the Scattered Homes.

work and cookery under the direction of the Yorkshire Ladies Council of Education'. The secretary had reported back to him that 'those that have attended this year have taken such an interest in their work and behaved so well that the teachers have quite enjoyed having them in their classes'. Some of the foster carers and the older boys and girls attended lectures on first aid which was to be repeated yearly. Cricket matches had been held at the headquarters and at Hillsborough Park which were reportedly very successful. He spoke about the fact that many applications had been received from people of Sheffield wishing to adopt the children: 'Twelve of the children had been adopted by fairly well-to-do persons who have seen the children in the homes.' There had been a similar interest in people wishing to apprentice the children, representing a great saving to the ratepayers.

The superintendent and his wife now assigned to the homes were Mr and Mrs Offen. The couple had been congratulated in August 1895 by the visiting committee for 'their ability in fulfilling their duties at the Scattered Homes of such a unique character. They had no model to follow which has led to them having to grope their way into getting some order and they have accomplished that very satisfactorily... and have loyally co-operated with the committee in turning the theory into a practical success.'

Three years later, on 20 October 1898, Mr and Mrs Offen applied for a raise in salary, which was agreed. Mr Wycliffe Wilson pointed out that the couple were to be congratulated 'for the great care and trouble they have exercised in training the children who had recently given entertainments in several schools in different parts of the city'. The couple were also praised for their diligence with the children, who had won prizes for basket making whilst under their care. It was also suggested by Mr Wycliffe Wilson that the children in the homes were in some cases superior to children in Sheffield itself. By July 1899 the Guardians were discussing a recent accident to Mr and Mrs Offen: the trap they had been driving had overturned, and as a result Mrs Offen had broken her spectacles and damaged some clothing. She was requesting £8 in compensation. Mr Young pointed out that workhouse officials were liable to accidents in the performance of their duty and questioned why the Guardians should pay the amount. The chair pointed out that it was the workhouse pony and trap which was driven by a workhouse inmate and felt that it was their responsibility to make good any damage. A vote was taken on it and the sum was agreed. It was generally accepted that Mr and Mrs Offen could do no wrong, but, as before with the Sheffield Guardians, things were about to change.

Rumblings started when a reply was printed in the local newspapers from the Prince of Wales' private secretary, Sir Francis Knollys, to a letter from Mr Offen on 22 October 1898. It seemed that a letter had been sent by Mr Offen to the Prince (later Edward VII) about the success of the Scattered Homes Scheme. At the Guardians' meeting, Mr R.B. Young announced that when he first read the printed reply he thought that it was a joke, as not one of the Guardians had authorized Mr Offen to send such a letter. The reply from the Prince had requested to know 'who the other gentlemen were who had worked with Mr and Mrs Offen in the development of the scheme'. Mr Young stated that it appears that Mr Offen had presented himself not as a workhouse officer but as a stipendiary Guardian involved in the decision making behind the scheme. He demanded that Mr Offen supply to the Guardians a copy of the letter which he had sent to the Prince of Wales. Mr Machon pointed out that if he had sent one of the leaflets which had been published a

Mr Offen, superintendent of Sheffield's Scattered Homes scheme.

short while before about the scheme then he was free to send it to whomever he pleased. The chair pointed out that if the letter was in return for one of those leaflets, the publishing costs of which had been met by several of the Guardians and by Mr Offen himself, then he was indeed entitled to send them out to anyone he thought suitable. Mr Wells Smith thought that the man was taking too much responsibility; Mr Offen's likeness had been at the front of the leaflet, and he was called 'the children's friend' in it. Mr Machon supported Mr Offen's stance and said to the chair that if they demanded that the original letter be produced they may as well ask him to produce his love letters, at which point there was much laughter in the Boardroom. Mr John Wilson told him to hold his tongue: 'as a new member I think the less he says the better'. At this point Mr Hoyland was about to speak, but before he could say anything Mr Wilson left his seat, saying, 'I am going. If you are going on, I won't stay to hear you, Samuel'. He was called to order by the chair but he ignored him and left the room. No resolution could be made and other business was then discussed and the meeting broke up shortly afterwards.

There is no further evidence in the Minutes as to whether it was a letter or a leaflet that had been sent to the Prince of Wales but at a later meeting, held on Wednesday, 17 November 1898, Mr Young proposed an amendment. He asked that Mr Offen refrain from using the term 'we' in any future correspondence, and that he add the title of his office to his signature. John Wilson seconded the amendment, which was carried. Mr Wycliffe Wilson felt that the amendment was unnecessary to a man who had only been doing his duty. The chair agreed and suggested that it was a very trivial matter. He asked the Board to withdraw the amendment. The matter was voted upon, and the amendment was withdrawn.

The Guardians were concerned to hear a disturbing report about a boy in November 1898: he had been sent out from one of the Cottage Homes to be apprenticed to a man, and the man had returned him to the workhouse about ten days previously, having taught him his trade. The only grievance he had was that the boy continually stayed out until after 10 p.m. at night. He had said that on one occasion the boy had come home late and had been rude to a servant, who had been instructed to wait up for him. Mr Wallace stated that 'if there were more cases of this sort it was evidence that the homes were not doing as well as they were given to understand.' Mr Wycliffe Wilson naturally rose to defend the scheme, telling his colleagues that he had been reported to be a 'very bad boy'. He had spoken to the committee and it was thought that the master was to blame and that the boy had been 'more sinned against than sinning'. He stated that: 'the scheme was not intended to turn out perfect any kind of boy that was received. Some of the worst material possible had to be dealt with and that it was extremely difficult to do so successfully. There were not the slightest grounds for suggesting that because one boy had turned out badly that the Homes scheme was a failure.'

Despite the evident success, it seemed that the Sheffield Cottage Homes scheme had been condemned in *The Times* of 2 June 1899. The president of the Local Government Board, Mr Chaplin, had made some remarks in the House of Commons which had been reported in *The Times* the following day. The gentleman had stated that the Board was always willing to give a full and fair trial to the Scattered Homes Scheme, but that 'the reports from the one at Sheffield were not encouraging'. He went on: 'that he could conceive nothing more deplorable than the fate of a child relegated to one of these homes, unkindly treated and regarded as something out of which a profit should be made'.

The Local Government Board pointed out that the newspaper had printed a condensed report of his speech which was about correct supervision of children in the care of Guardians. What he had actually said was that 'there had been reports on Sheffield Scattered Homes which in some respects were not so satisfactory as might be desirable'. They stated that Mr Chaplin had no intention of casting aspersions on the Sheffield Board of Guardians, who had been a pioneer of a movement which was most thoroughly deserving of encouragement. The Guardians felt that all the reports made upon the scheme which had been sent to the Local Government Board had been of a very positive nature. The chair resolved that the clerk write a letter to the Board asking them to give an 'authoritive explanation' for implying that the reports from Sheffield were unsatisfactory. They requested that if the Board could suggest any way of making improvements the Guardians would be pleased to implement such suggestions, and that Mr Chaplin visit the Sheffield Scattered Homes Scheme to see it for himself. The resolution was carried unanimously.

The Sheffield Guardians were not afraid to try out new and experimental schemes, which they adopted with great enthusiasm and energy. Removing the children from the workhouse was applauded by the Local Government Board, and there is little doubt that its success led to the setting up of other such homes in the towns of Yorkshire. These homes were the forerunners of Cottage Homes adopted by Group Captain Cheshire for people with disabilities, where individuals could live together as families. However, for the rest of the inhabitants of the Sheffield workhouse, life was very different, and the stigma of being in the workhouse – and the terror of being forced into it – led to the institution being viewed with suspicion and with a fear that was not totally unfounded.

eleven

The Dark Side of the Workhouse

Workhouses were meant to deter the poor, and one of the largest fears for the inmates was the manner of their deaths and burials under the workhouse authorities. The stories and rumours which grew up around the Poor Law sometimes had their origins in facts. Whilst the long-held belief that workhouse bread was poisoned to keep down the numbers of the poor was easily dispelled, the fact that unclaimed paupers' bodies could be used for dissection was less easily dismissed. By 1820, the shortage of bodies for medical students to study was causing a problem. On 27 June 1829, the medical professions of Sheffield petitioned Parliament to remove the difficulties which obstructed the study of anatomy. This petition was ignored, as they again petitioned in April 1828 and in February of 1830. As a much-needed commodity, corpses could be sold to the medical community for up to £10, and this brought out people who would dig up bodies from recent graves, the 'Resurrectionists', in force. A Bill for the Sale of Human Bodies was introduced before Parliament in 1829 but it was very unpopular. The previous year had seen the famous trial of Burke and Hare, whose atrocities as bodysnatchers in Edinburgh in December 1828 had horrified the nation and brought the term 'burke', meaning to murder for sale, into general usage. Yet the medical schools were clamouring for bodies for students to dissect. In 1832 the Anatomy Act was passed: it agreed that any paupers' body which lay unclaimed in the workhouse could be used for dissection. The system was reviled in the *Sheffield Iris* on Tuesday, 9 June 1829: 'the Act gives the overseers of the workhouses, whose abuse of power under the Poor Law system has become a crying grievance, the additional privilege of selling bodies and opening a market in every workhouse for the sale of human bodies.'

There was a general outcry in Sheffield: people feared that if they died in poverty in the Kelham Street workhouse their bodies would be dissected. Such was the indignation against this law that, on 25 January 1835, there were riots at the Sheffield medical school in Eyre Street. It was reported that large crowds assembled at the school after rumours began to circulate that some students and teachers were about to 'burke' a woman. There were cries of 'murder' and the doors to the school were forced open. The mob flooded into the dissecting rooms, where they found the body of a woman with injuries around her neck. The body of a man which had been partly dissected – and his bowels and other

Dissecting room of Sheffield Medical School, where rioters found a body that had been 'burked'.

parts of his body removed – was seen by the mob, which fuelled them even more. It was later reported in the newspaper that the body still had one of his stockings on his feet. The windows were smashed and shouts of 'burn and destroy' were heard, but the police managed to gain entrance into the medical school. Two men, Thomas Staniforth and James Ogden, were arrested, but later acquitted. As night fell, all the Sheffield watchmen were employed in maintaining a vigilant presence. On Monday morning, between 7 a.m. and 8 a.m., the medical school was broken into once again, and anything moveable was either thrown out of the windows or set on fire. The clerk to the local magistrate sent a letter to a Justice of the Peace, Mr W.J. Bagshaw Esq., to inform him of events, and the Chief Constable, Mr Raynor, sent a letter to the barracks asking for a military force to be sent to the medical school. Meanwhile, at 9.30 a.m. a fire engine arrived to put out the fire, but it was received by 'a storm of stones and brickbats' and forced to retreat. A detachment of Inniskillen Dragoons entered the top of Eyre Street, and after the Riot Act had been read by Mr Bagshaw they dispersed the crowd and the fire was extinguished. The medical school was completely gutted, but the good citizens of Sheffield had not finished yet. They managed to enter the school once again to fire the remains, determined to ensure that the hated place was destroyed. The military were once again called out: they galloped down Eyre Street and the mob fled in all directions.

Newspaper reports verified that the unclaimed bodies of paupers from the Kelham Street workhouse could be dissected at the medical school. There are no reports of what emotional effect this had on the paupers of the workhouse, but it must have made an enormous impact. The letter book reveals that the practice of collecting the bodies was for the master to notify the medical school when a body was available: the porter of the school would then go to Kelham Street and collect it. In November 1847 one of the surgeons, Samuel Gregory, wrote to the master enclosing some forms for him to complete. He wrote: 'Dear Sir, I have forwarded you half a dozen notices and medical certificates which I trust you will have the kindness to fill up as usual and we should be very glad to receive any unclaimed bodies. You will perceive at the back of the notice is an abstract from the Anatomy Act which is required to be carried out under the strict letter of the law. We hope to receive the benefit of your confirmation as heretofore.'

Mr Rogers notified Mr Gregory on Christmas Eve that they had another unclaimed body, belonging to a man named Robert Trueman who had died on the night of 20 December 1847. By 1859 it was noted by George Kershaw, the Inspector of Anatomy for the Provinces, that the supply of unclaimed bodies from Kelham Street workhouse had been less than in previous years and he wrote to Mr Rogers that he was 'hoping for a continuance of his kind co-operation'. He stated that he hoped the lesser number of bodies 'had not arisen from any unwillingness to give up the unclaimed bodies'.

The body was generally transported to the school in a cab. It was pointed out to the Guardians in 1846 that an Act of Parliament required the body to be placed in a coffin or shell before removal for dissection, and that it should afterwards be 'decently interred'. The Act required that the onus of providing the coffin or shell was with the persons giving up the body, and that therefore it was the responsibility of the Guardians to provide it. The Guardians disagreed, stating that it was the medical school that should provide the coffin. This they finally agreed to do. They requested that the visiting committee draw up regulations as to the removal of bodies from Kelham Street workhouse and gain the assent of the medical school to them before allowing any more bodies to be removed. One of the Guardians, a Mr Harvey, requested in June 1862 that more effort be put into tracing the friends or relatives of unclaimed bodies: it often taken for granted, he said, that a poor creature dying at the workhouse had no friends because no one claimed the body. The chair suggested that the master, Mr Westcoe, report the bodies given up for dissection to the Guardians or the visiting committee and the committee enquire into what steps had been taken to identify any friends of the dead paupers. Needless to say, the inmates had the least say in the matter, although it was agreed that if a pauper stated clearly that he did not want to be dissected then his wishes would be adhered to. However, it was pointed out that it was very difficult for anyone to ask a pauper on his deathbed whether they would allow it or not. Mr Crawshaw suggested that the dissected bodies be returned to the workhouse so that the Guardians could ensure they had a Christian burial, which

Masters' note to medical school regarding the unclaimed body of Robert Trueman.

was carried unanimously. Despite this, the following week it was agreed that the medical school would be responsible for the burial – and further, that instead of the master telling the medical school when a body was available, the medical school should apply to the Guardians when in need of one. They resolved that:

- The secretary of the Medical School be required to send a written notice to the master of the workhouse when a body is required for anatomical lectures. That such a notice be kept in a book for that purpose.
- That the master having an unclaimed dead body shall after using every endeavour and making every enquiry to ascertain the existence of relatives of the deceased, and failing to find any, shall give up such body to the officers of the Medical School entering the particulars as to name, age, cause of death and the date of giving up in the same book as that in which the application is inserted.
- From the passing of these rules no dead body shall be given up for anatomical purposes or shall be allowed to leave the workhouse other than in a proper coffin paid for by the Medical School.
- That the secretary of the Medical School be prepared to certify to the master of the workhouse within six weeks after receiving a body from the workhouse that such body be interred in a proper coffin, the date and place of the interment and that the Burial Service had been duly performed together with the name of the officiating clergyman such certificate to be signed by the secretary of the Medical School and the officiating clergyman.
- That the master lay the certificate before the visiting committee after receiving the same, and then file it.

It was originally agreed that the master be the one responsible for signing the paperwork until it was pointed out to the Guardians in July of 1862 that they were the ones in the possession of the paupers' bodies and that all paperwork must be signed by them. The Guardians needed clear guidelines about the collection of unclaimed bodies after a shocking scandal broke out at St Phillips Churchyard, where corpses had been discovered in a stable belonging to the sexton and the vicar had been accused of burying the remains of dissected corpses without a proper burial service. (For more information, see my recent collection *Sheffield Crimes: A Gruesome Selection of Victorian Cases*.)

The Victorians believed strongly that the ritual of burial must be approached with great dignity and that the bodies of both rich and poor should be dealt with sensitively. In January of 1882 the Guardian's worst fears were realised: an embarrassing mix-up of bodies occurred, one of which had been sent for dissection. An inquiry was held at Fir Vale workhouse into the case of the body of John Wood, aged thirty-six, which had been taken to the medical school for dissection instead of that of John Ellis, aged seventy-one. The enquiry, held before Mr Basil Cane on Monday, 30 January 1882, ensured that the above regulations were read out, but the master, Mr John Archibald Heastie, stated that he had only seen those regulations on 13 March of the previous year. What he usually did was to first enquire whether the deceased had any friends; then he notified the licensed teacher of the school of anatomy that there was a body available. The body would be left in the dead house whilst he received the death certificate from the Medical Officer. On this occasion the body was transported to the school in a hearse which was in the charge of two of the inmates. Possibly fearing an outcry and criticism in the local press, the master revealed that there had been 400 deaths since he had been appointed master but that he had only sent twelve pauper bodies for dissection in that time. After dissection the bodies were then decently buried and the costs paid for by the school of anatomy. In the case of Thomas Ellis, who died on 18 January 1882, the master had made enquiries in the usual way. He had kept the body for five days, which was longer than usual, and then gave directions for the body to be removed to the medical school. Dr Hunt, the Medical Officer, told him to send it as he had been informed that they were short of bodies at the school. When asked who was in charge of ensuring that the bodies were transported to the school in a shell, he stated that it was usually left to inmates in charge of the dead house. The master told the enquiry that he had seen Mrs Wood on his way to the dead house, who told him that her husband's body had been removed. He looked in the coffin, clearly labelled 'Mr Wood, aged 36', and found the body of Ellis. He immediately sent a message to the medical school to stop the dissection, and the body was returned. It was found that Wood had been shaved but his body was intact. Only a small amount of preservative fluid in the upper part of the chest had been inserted, but nothing untoward could be seen by his wife.

From the enquiry it appeared that a number of inmates were responsible for separate parts of the delivery of the bodies. Edward Hamilton, an inmate who was assigned to the dead house, gave evidence that when the bodies were removed from the wards they did not always have labels on them. The plates for the coffins would be made at the joiner's shop. He was not responsible for placing the bodies inside the coffins, although he was responsible for screwing down the lids and making sure that the plate was put on the coffin. He had not looked at the body in the coffin before putting on the lid. William Colishaw, another inmate, said that the body of Ellis had been brought to the dead house by a nurse from the ward. The body was placed in a coffin with the lid off. He did not see the lid being screwed down. He was discharged from the dead house by the master on Monday and did not return to it again. He stated that Wood's body was not in the dead house whilst he was there.

Eliza Wood, the widow of the deceased, residing in West Street, next gave evidence. She stated that she had seen her husband's body at the workhouse in a shell on the previous Saturday. The next time she saw it was on Tuesday, when some visiting friends from Manchester asked to see him before he was interred. She said that the body was now in a coffin with his name plate on. When the coffin was opened, however, she saw that it was the wrong man. The master told her there had been a mistake, but that if she returned back to the workhouse at 7 p.m. she would be able to see her husband. The master did not tell her that her husband's body had been taken to the medical school. When she went back to the workhouse she had to wait for the body of her husband, which was returned at 7.30 p.m. Mr Edward Skinner, lecturer on anatomy and a licensed teacher to the medical school, apologised for the mix-up between the bodies and assured her that nothing had been done on the body before returning it apart from the shaving and the injection.

Mr Cane concluded the enquiry by announcing that he would submit his report to the Local Government Board, who would pronounce judgment on the whole affair, and that 'no one could regret more than himself and the Guardians that this unfortunate mistake had happened because it brought pain, wretchedness and misery on the persons concerned and to a certain extent brought opprobrium on an establishment which was usually so well conducted and generally deserved the highest praise.'

Mr Cane was later been criticised for his handling of the enquiry, which had occupied more than seven hours: the Guardians accused him of browbeating the master and not allowing witnesses to be fully questioned. One of the Guardians, Mr Bartholomew, came from the same village as Ellis and knew him quite well. He questioned the amount of enquiries which had been made about relatives, as he was aware that Ellis had friends and relatives in the village (though he agreed that they were distant relatives). The assistant master had been told to write to some of these relatives and had written two letters, on 16 and 19 January, to which he had no reply. The matter was then dropped. However, within days rumours were circulating the town that before the rule of the present master the paupers were buried in old shirts instead of shrouds. The chair indignantly retorted that this was 'just not true' and said that such stories reflected badly on the Guardians themselves. Nevertheless, a letter had been written to the master in October 1848 at the behest of Revd M. Blackburn, who asked the master 'if it was customary to inter paupers from the workhouse without any covering'. The letter, signed Mr George Sykes, states that two coffins had been opened and the dead bodies inside 'found quite naked' and without a shroud.

On Saturday, 12 March 1864 the Kelham Street workhouse was needed to store 124 bodies of people who had been killed in the Sheffield Flood. Just after midnight on Friday

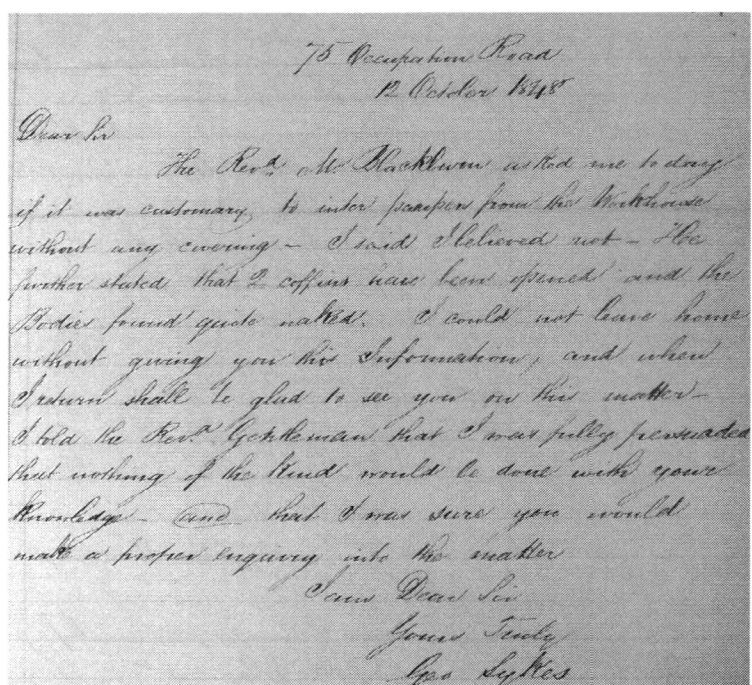

Letter regarding naked bodies buried without a shroud.

11 March the newly built Dale Dyke dam burst, sending thousands of gallons of water down the Loxley and the Don Valley and into the town of Sheffield itself. Houses and factories were swept away, leaving a trail of destruction and death in the water's wake. The water had flooded into the rooms of the workhouse on Kelham Street and the massive gates and barred doors had been forced open by the impact of the water. In some rooms the water had risen to the height of several feet. The flood had been spotted by a man in charge of the boiler house. He roused the officers by whistling and shouting and took his place on the roof of the building. Twenty able-bodied men were roused and sent across to rescue the paupers from the two wards in the most critical places; they contained children suffering from measles and smallpox and the female venereal wards. The flood by this time had risen to the underneath of the beds, but no lives were lost in the workhouse and the rescued paupers were removed to the upper part of the female hospital. The bodies of those who had been drowned started to come in about 3 a.m. and continued over the next few days. Of the 124 bodies recovered, there had been sixty-nine males and fifty-five females and children; 102 of these bodies had been identified and twenty-three were still unclaimed the following week. The 124 bodies of the people who had died in the flood were collected at the workhouse; they were cleaned and laid out for friends and relatives to claim. It was reported that sixty-eight bodies were removed by relatives and fifty-six were interred at the expense of the union. Several of the Guardians, upon hearing of the disaster, made their way to the workhouse in order to deal with requests for relief and to give advice to those who had lost relatives or friends. The Guardians worked tirelessly from the early hours of Saturday morning to Tuesday evening. The chair reported that he had been one of the first Guardians on the scene and that every officer and pauper that had been involved 'performed their duty in the most admirable manner'. He also praised the work of the master, Mr Westcoe, and the matron, Miss Day, for the tireless way in which they had acted during this terrible catastrophe.

At the time of the Guardians' meetings on Wednesday 16 March the chair informed the group that he had been in contact with the Poor Law Board and they had agreed that temporary relief could be given, but not, as yet, money to replace clothing or belongings. They were to make appropriate records of all relief given. The master reported that there was quite a crowd of people in the entrance hall and Mr Muddiman and Mr Hallam agreed to address the crowds below and let them know what was happening. Mr Hallam

The devastation caused by the Sheffield Flood on housing on the Wicker.

told them that there were, at that time, twelve committees preparing to administer relief for them. Many of the assembled victims left, but they were quickly replaced by others. Mr Mainwaring from the Poor Law Board had visited the chair, and told him that if the Board needed anything at all they were to contact him even on 'matters that were not strictly according to orders'. He had advised taking on assistants to help the relieving officers, but as committees were being set up to meet the immediate needs of the victims of the flood, he thought it unnecessary. Gradually the life of the pauper inmates got back to normal and by the following week all the lower rooms and yards had been cleaned and whitewashed and – apart from a few cases of diarrhoea – the workhouse had returned to full health. The following year, on 28 September 1864, the water company paid the workhouse some compensation for the damage done to the building, amounting to £328 16s 2d (which included £50 for coffins and burials). They rejected paying the remaining part of the claim, for £90 17s 9d, on the grounds that this was the sum of relief given. Some discussion took place on this, but the chair gloomily surmised that they had no legal grounds to recover relief given to destitute persons from those who caused that destitution. Appealing to the Poor Law Board was suggested, but this was rejected on the grounds that they might get a lesser amount than the water company offered. It was therefore agreed to accept the offered amount with good grace.

It seems that for many years it was the custom for the coroner to have all bodies of people who committed suicide taken to the workhouse and there to be buried by the workhouse authorities. In September of 1864 the practice was strongly criticised by the chair to the Board of Guardians. It seems that the body of such a person, a woman named Pritchett of whom the inquest verdict had been of *felo de se* (self murder or suicide), had been brought to the workhouse. The chair, Mr Saunders, strongly criticised the manner of internment which the coroner had required. It seems that all persons who had this, now outdated, verdict had to be buried at night and in unconsecrated ground. There was no dignity at these funerals, which were normally accompanied by cat calls and scenes of revelry, and it was felt that to have removed the body from where she died at Silver Street would have created a great disturbance. The union clerk told him that an old law empowered the coroner to have all bodies of people found dead in the streets or who committed suicide to be given to the overseers and taken to the workhouse for burial. The chair stated that 'such practice of a dark and barbarous age ought not in the present age be sanctioned in any way by the Guardians or carried out by their servants. There was a strong feeling in the town against such usages all together.'

Nevertheless, only a few months later, in January 1865, there was another suicide and the inquest was held at the Steers Hotel. After the inquest the coroner, Mr John Webster Esq., had sent an order to the master to remove and inter the body. Mr Westcoe asked one of the Guardians what he should do: he was told to do it, and that the chair would deal with the matter later. The chair then wrote to the coroner:

High Street 18 Jan 1865
Dear Sir,
The master of Sheffield workhouse has sent to me an order from you the coroner to bury the body of an unknown man found dead. I have told the master to comply on this

occasion with the order. I shall however be glad if in future you make the order on the proper parties, the overseers. Neither the Guardians nor the master of the workhouse have anything to do with the unknown man found dead in the town. If a request to oblige you in future is sent, no doubt the Guardians will willingly aid you, but no order in future can be complied with and no further bodies, save those of our own poor, can be received into the workhouse.

I remain truly yours,

George L. Saunders

The coroner replied stating that he sent an order 'as the law requires me to sign to the workhouse where I have hitherto supposed the business of the township as regards the poor is transacted'. He added, somewhat sanctimoniously, that he shall 'ask no favour of the Guardians'. Mr Saunders informed the other members of the Board that he had also sent a note to Mr Jackson, the Chief Constable, to state that bodies of people found dead should not be sent to the workhouse in future but should instead be left where they are or taken to the nearest and most convenient house.

The Guardians may have objected to having to bury the bodies of suicides, but they had no option but to bury the dead bodies of any inmates from the workhouse. Pauper burials had long been the subject of much criticism in the local press, in particular relating to the state of the coffins. In May 1873 two complaints about the workhouse coffins were received by the editor of the local newspaper. This was following the interment of the body of a man found drowned in the canal at Attercliffe. The letters had been written to the *Sheffield Independent* and one was from Mr Roebuck of Woodburn Road, Attercliffe and the other from Revd John Calvert. The complaint made by Mr Roebuck had been that the coffin for the man had been too short and that the body, as a consequence, could not be put into it. Revd Calvert complained that when he interred the body he found it was the merest shell that scarcely held together and that the corpse could distinctly be seen as the shell was lowered into the ground. The chair commented that he wished that members of the public who had a complaint would make it to the Board of Guardians rather than the press.

Upon examination it was discovered that when the corpse was found, Mr Jackson, the relieving officer, ordered a coffin from the undertaker who supplied the workhouse. He also sent a message to the master asking him to supply the workhouse hearse. The men who took the hearse called at the undertakers' but found the coffin was too small. They returned it for another one – which was once again too small. Eventually they managed to squeeze the body inside and took it to the cemetery. Due to the absence of Mr Bramwell, the secretary of the Attercliffe Burial Board, no grave had been dug, and the coffin was left in the chapel overnight. The following morning, due to the body being in the water for so long, the body had swelled, which in turn distorted the coffin. The chair pointed out that it was the duty of the overseers to bury the bodies of persons found dead, but often the relieving officers had taken over that duty as a matter of convenience. Mr Jackson was called before the Board. He told them that he had given a verbal order for the coffin, which was usual in these matters, and that 'he did not consider it any portion of his duty to measure the corpse'. He had also sent a message to Mr Bramwell to have a

A CASE FOR THE WORKHOUSE OFFICIALS.

To the Editor,—Sir, will you give me space in your paper to call the attention of the workhouse authorities to a disgraceful scene? A man no one could identify was found dead in the canal on Monday at noon, and was taken to the Woodburn Hotel, Bacon Lane, where the inquest was held on Wednesday. On Thursday six old men came with the hearse to fetch the corpse away. They attempted to put the body in the coffin, but only the legs would go in, the head lay on the edge, and the arms hung over the sides, and the body was put in the hearse in this style, nothing to cover it with. Perhaps the authorities will say through your columns what has become of the body? Surely we pay rates sufficient to have the dead put away respectfully. Trusting the matter will be seen to,

Yours, &c.,

           WILLIAM ROEBUCK,
           Bacon Lane, Attercliffe.

May 9th, 1873.

THE CASE FOR THE WORKHOUSE OFFICIALS.

To the Editor.—The body of the unidentified man found in the canal last Monday was interred by me on Friday in Attercliffe Cemetery. The scene at the funeral was little less repulsive and disgraceful than that to which your correspondent Mr. Roebuck refers after the inquest. The coffin appeared the merest shell, the handles of which were broken, and the lid of which did not close in the middle by three inches. The corpse itself was distinctly seen, and it appeared to me that it was only by the great care of the sexton, and the two old men from the workhouse who assisted him, that the coffin held together while the body was lowered into the grave. The authorities, I am sure, only need their attention directing to these revolting details to see to it that such a scene shall not again be witnessed.—Yours truly,

           JOHN CALVERT.

Attercliffe, May 10th, 1873.

Revd Roebuck and Mr Calvert's letters regarding the state of workhouse coffins.

grave ready for 3 p.m., but in his absence the message had not been delivered. It was resolved that a vote of censure be carried to Mr Jackson and the vote was four to two against. The state of the coffins had been a cause for complaint seven years previously when it was noted that the undertaker had taken 12s from a friend and relative of a workhouse inmate to replace the badly fitting workhouse coffin for a much better one.

The following week one of the Guardians, Mr Bacon, criticised not only the coffins but also the manner of burial of inmates from the workhouse. He remarked that about a month previously he had been at the Sheffield General Cemetery and witnessed the burial of three paupers from the workhouse. He told his colleagues that every one of the coffins was split across the top. He had also noted that the paupers carrying the coffins were old and infirm and hardly able to bear the weight of the coffins. Another Guardian commented that the coffins were often too narrow, and that was why they split. The Guardians resolved to have a stock of coffins kept at the workhouse to ensure they were properly constructed. It was also agreed that larger coffins needed to be made in order to prevent such matters being brought to the Boardroom again. Thankfully, by July 1895 Messrs Foxon and Roberts, the contractors for coffins, were charging the Guardians 2s for children and 2s 6d for adults for measuring the bodies and putting them into the coffins (which were then costing 7s 6d each). However, the cheapness of the coffins must have made a deep impression on the people of the workhouse. Just a few months later, in December 1895, an unnamed inmate had left a sum of money with a Mrs Dimelow of Bridgehouses in order for her to bury him in a 'private coffin' at his death. Unfortunately, it was reported to the Guardians that the man had already died and been buried from the workhouse in the usual manner before she got to hear about it. On informing the receiving officer the sum of money, amounting to £2 16s, was handed to the collector for the man's maintenance in the Fir Vale workhouse. The disparity of costs does tend to indicate that the coffins were probably of the cheapest design and that the fears for many paupers at the workhouse were found to be deserved. One coroner, Mr D. Wightman, also criticised the Guardians – not for the state of the coffins this time, but for the state of the body. An inquest was held on the remains of Ellen Wright in July 1894. Wightman told the Guardians that the jury had drawn his attention to the body of the deceased; Ellen

Sheffield General Cemetery, where workhouse paupers were buried in coffins which were split and in poor condition.

had been a workhouse inmate, and had been reported to be 'in a filthy state'. The Medical Officer was called before the Guardians and he reported that 'everything that could be done for her had been done during her lifetime'. But he admitted that 'her body showed signs of pests which is so difficult to eradicate in a dying person'.

From research it also seems that although many of the paupers were buried in the Sheffield Cemetery, they were usually buried in unconsecrated parts of the grounds. A letter was received by the Guardians in June 1861 from Revd Greville Chester, the incumbent of Moorfield, complaining that a member of his church had been a young man called Frederick Day. The man had been a patient in the Kelham Street hospital and after a long illness 'borne with patience' he had died in March 1861. When Revd Chester attended the grave he found it was in a part of the churchyard that was unconsecrated. He was told that it was the practice to bury paupers without the service for the dead according to the rites of the church. He informed the Guardians that he was intending to write to the Poor Law Board but asked them for their comments before he did. The Guardians discussed the case and considered ignoring the matter, but eventually the following letter was sent:

> In reply to your note Frederick Day was admitted on 17 November 1860 and died 30 March 1861. He gave his religion as Protestant. No order is given to officers conveying the body to the cemetery nor are instructions given where they should be buried as it is a matter of perfect indifference to them. However if a preference for a site of burial is given the Guardians will do their utmost to comply with that request.

The reason for burying the inmates in unconsecrated grounds was probably financial. We know that the cost of burials to the Guardians was 8s in 1857. The Guardians reported in March 1862 that they now paid an extra 2s 3d per body for the inmates to be buried in a consecrated part of the cemetery – which they complained was over £100 per year, as there had been 539 burials the previous year.

This dismissive way in which pauper burials were carried out is typical of the way in which the poor were seen and treated by the Poor Law and its officials. It also indicates the cause of the fear experienced by most paupers who died in the workhouses. There are no records of any pauper expressing a preference for the manner of his burial or funeral rites. But the Guardians would have had to consider the expenses involved and it is unlikely that a better coffin would be provided or a lengthy service would be held. At a time when Victorian funeral rites were carried out to the letter regarding length of mourning, and the service itself designed for the middle and upper classes, no regard was paid to the needs of the paupers and their last rites. A poem which was written during this period put it most succinctly: 'Rattle his bones over the stones. He's only a pauper that nobody owns.'

twelve

Imbeciles and Lunatics

The public attitude to mental health issues began to change in the Victorian era as doctors investigated better treatment for 'imbeciles and lunatics'. This was partly a result of the 1845 Lunacy Act, which required lunatic hospitals to be inspected by government officials on a regular basis. Lunatics could no longer be held in workhouses and now had to be sent to specialised hospitals for treatment. The Victorians, with their love of classification, separated patients into two categories: there were imbeciles who were non-violent and might be expected to undertake simple tasks around the workhouse, and more violent lunatics who were sent to asylums for treatment (such as Wadsley Lunatic Asylum or the West Riding Lunatic Asylum at Wakefield). The reality was that imbeciles who were unable to work and earn their own living might be used in workhouses in whatever capacity they were capable of meeting. This usually meant in the laundry, kitchen or in hospital wards. In the Sheffield workhouse letter book there is a list of patients in April of 1850 at the Wadsley Lunatic Asylum who were being paid for by ratepayers of Sheffield. They include:

Hannah Greensmith	George Smith	Mary Gambles
John Barber	Charles Barker	Frances Hinchcliffe
Job Stevenson	John Smith	Elizabeth Taylor
John Parkin	Hannah Truelove	Hannah Renshaw
Ellen Cutts	Ellen Baines	Dorothy Cooper
George Woolley	Septimus Shaw	John Burkinshaw
Ann Hibberd	Selina Wilson	Ann Gill
Sophia Ardron	Robert Tomlinson	Mary H. Maleham
Thomas Knowles	Ann Chapman	Mary Elston
George Pulfrey	Jonas Smith	Timothy Smith
Henry Pye	John Roper	

Those patients that were paid for by the Sheffield ratepayers but came from Brightside Bierlow were listed as:

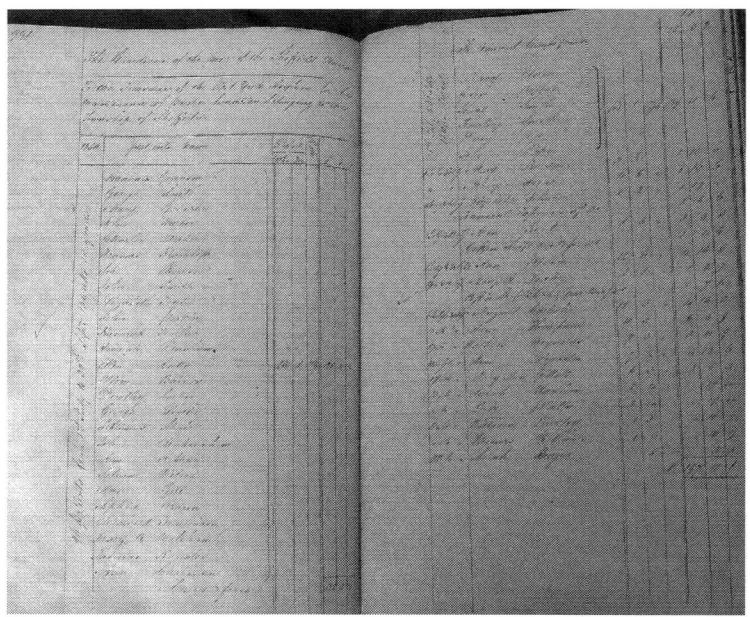

Lists of lunatics at South Yorkshire Asylum (Wadsley).

Mary Linley	Henry Jackson	George Auglity
Elizabeth Wardle	Martha Newton	David Stones
Mary Booth	Mary Jackson	Joseph Bagshaw

Patients from Attercliffe cum Darnall were listed as:

Ann Goodine	Elizabeth Acland	Mary Hargreaves
Mary Beaver	Joseph Varley	

We know that in the workhouses of Kelham Street and Fir Vale lunatics and imbeciles were kept in the 'retreat wards'. The treatment of these patients was very basic, as little was known about the causes or effects of mental illness. For example, we see that in June 1861 forty-eight of the inhabitants of this ward included epileptics. Maybe the Guardians were beginning to understand the futility of having epileptics in the retreat wards by February of 1891, as a man named Henry Wilson then asked to be discharged from the asylum if the Guardians allowed him medicine from the dispensary. He told them that the only reason he was in the workhouse was due to his fits, and it was agreed, providing the Medical Officer sanctioned the man leaving. The retreat wards also included patients suffering from the effects of alcohol. One such patient, who died there on the night of 19 December 1847, was a man named William Fowler, admitted with *delirium tremens*. The master informed the Chief Constable, Mr Raynor, that he had been treated there by Dr Deakin, and that the deceased man had a sister living at 55 Town Head Street, Purseglove.

Another patient died in these wards a few days later. The master notified Mr Raynor that she was Eliza Warburton, aged about thirty-four, who had 'been an inmate of the retreat ward for many years'. She had died the previous evening about 11 p.m. and was described as:

A quiet harmless idiot, quite useless in society and devoid of those propensities to violence so often exhibited by that class. She has been ill for some weeks and has been attended by the surgeon and every kindness shown to her. As soon as you have the warrant for the inquest I shall be glad if you let me know the time. I am not able to ascertain whether she had any relatives or friends as no one ever saw any and there is none recorded in the books.

We do know that restraints were used for the more violent patients as there is a note in the letter book from a Medical Officer, John Shaw, requesting to borrow the 'strait waistcoat' on Christmas Day, 1847. The use of restraints was being questioned in a report which was presented to the Guardians on 25 March 1869. The Commissioner declared:

The padded room was rarely used although it was sometimes used for fits and there were two restraining chairs in each ward which patients are locked in. In my opinion I think these chairs should be removed and broken up but if they must remain the master should be the person to have the key and every case of restraint should be sanctioned by the Medical Officer as is the case with strait jackets.

The following year the master told Mr Raynor about the death of David Cryer, aged twenty-one, who had been found dead in his bed that morning. He also had been an inmate of the retreat wards for many years and was subject to peculiar fits which were preceded by 'violent and ungovernable conduct'. He noted that prior to the attack he was of robust health. He appears to have died during a fit, turning on his face in bed and suffocating; he was found dead at 6.45 a.m.

The Sheffield Guardians requested that the Medical Officers list all the cases in the retreat wards in June 1896. These lists indicate the lack of knowledge about the subject, as many of the causes would be treated very differently today. The Medical Officer listed forty-two cases of dementia and senile dementia, twenty-eight imbeciles, seventeen cases of general paralysis, eleven of delusional and ten of acute mania. Other diagnosis involved religious mania, suicidal mania, melancholia and alcoholism. Another case which illustrates the lack of understanding around these issues was recorded on 14 June 1865. It seems that a girl called Broadbent had been brought to the workhouse in a dying state. She had been admitted to the Sheffield Infirmary previously suffering from bronchitis and fever, and it was there she became delirious. A relative, Mrs Hawthorne, had taken the girl to the Infirmary at 11 a.m. on the day in question, and she later complained to the Guardians that she had not been seen by a surgeon until after 1 p.m. At 9 p.m., Mrs Hawthorne had been sent for and was told to take the girl home as her hysterical fits were disturbing the other patients. When she asked what she should do if the girl became delirious again she was informed to 'throw a bucket of cold water over her'. They also told her to get her into the workhouse lunatic ward the following day. Mrs Hawthorne brought the girl to the workhouse the following morning wrapped in blankets in a cab; she was found to be insensible when she arrived, and she died the next day. The treatment of this poor girl indicates the attitude of even trained medical staff to the requirements of people with mental-health needs, and is quite appalling.

The use of imbeciles as ward nurses inevitably led to tragedy, illustrated in the death of a lunatic which was reported in the *Sheffield Free Press* for 22 January 1853. The inquest was heard at the workhouse in front of the coroner, T. Badger Esq., on the body of George Palfrey. Palfrey had spent the previous thirty years as a resident of both the Sheffield workhouse and the Wakefield Asylum. Palfrey had been placed under the care of another lunatic and stole away to the privy in the middle of the night. His body was found the following day suspended from the rafters by his neckerchief, his feet being only an inch or so off the ground. The coroner heard all the evidence and the jury's verdict was that he had 'hung himself whilst in a state of insanity'. It was not until 1861 that a superintendent and his wife, Mr and Mrs Nicks, were made responsible for the supervision of the inmates of the retreat wards.

Following the 1845 Lunacy Act, the lunatic wards of workhouses and asylums were inspected by a Commissioner for Lunacy on a regular basis and reports were given to the Guardians and the Poor Law authorities. There were several complaints that the Guardians were keeping lunatics at the Kelham Street workhouse longer than was necessary. In August 1858 the Poor Law Board drew the attention to the Guardians of the report of one of the Commissioners, Mr B. F. Proctor, who had visited the workhouse on 5 August. He complained about the fact that lunatics had not been sent to the asylum 'despite the Acts of Parliament now in force'. He demanded that Andrew Loxley, who was reported to be 'violently insane', should be sent to an asylum 'as soon as the fever under which he is now labouring will permit'. Another case, that of Caroline Johnson who was insane, sleepless and 'very much excited', should, he felt, go to an asylum as soon as possible. They wrote to the Poor Law Board and assured them that Caroline Johnson, who had only been admitted to the workhouse a few days previously, 'had already gone to the asylum and Andrew Loxley would be sent as soon as the Medical Officer thought that he was fit enough'. The Guardians added that 'whilst being fully alive to the responsibility resting upon them they also believe that they have amply met every requirement and they object to the retention of any but the most harmless lunatic in the workhouse.'

The condition of patients in the retreat wards of Kelham Street was revealed in a report written by a Commissioner Campbell, who visited Sheffield in December 1860. At that time he reports there were sixty-three people who were classed as 'lunatics' or 'idiots'. Of these, there were nineteen males and twenty-one females in the retreat ward, the rest being in other parts of the house. The Commissioner admitted that he inspected all of them who looked clean and healthy. None were restrained or isolated and none were in 'an excited condition', but he was critical of the fact that although the women were occupied with their needle and doing domestic work, the men had nothing to occupy them at all. He also criticized the fact that the bathrooms for both sexes were placed in an outside yard instead of being within the separate wards themselves. As he pointed out, access to these bathrooms would have been difficult for aged or infirm lunatics. He also condemned the fact that the wishes of the Poor Law Board had been overruled regarding the erection of a new workhouse and states:

In these circumstances it is my duty to protest against the use of the present lunatic wards as a place for permanent residence of insane paupers. They are in every way unfit for the purpose and no alterations can render them suitable owing to their confined and gloomy situation. I think therefore that all patients who cannot be mixed with others should be sent to the asylum… Placed as there are at present with no amusement, occupation or interest of any kind and with very insufficient means for exercise there is no hope of any improvement taking place. On the contrary, the most rapid deterioration of mind and body can only be anticipated.

The chair criticised the report as being very contradictory. He told his colleagues that Mr Campbell praised the fact that all the people appeared well and that no criticism was offered to the Medical Officer or the master at the time of his visit. He pointed out that a total of seventy-four inmates had been sent home or to their friends as being cured due to their care within the retreat wards. Nevertheless, we are left with an image of these wards as confined and gloomy, which would have added to the wretchedness of the people placed there. The wards were criticised again by Mr Campbell the following year, in August 1861, as being totally unsuitable for that purpose. Even though Mr and Mrs Nicks were by this point supervising the wards, he reported that: 'The retreat wards are now under the supervision of a superintendent and his wife whose joint salary is only £45 a year. At times of need they are helped out by paupers who get extra rations for the work. There were no chairs in the day room or in the dormitory. These and other comfortable furniture is much needed by the inmates.'

He comments that although the men still have no exercise or activities he was glad to hear that groups of either sex were now being taken out once a week by the superintendent and his wife. But he criticised the Guardians once again for the fact that lunatics were being kept at the workhouse. The Guardians were stung by his comments but the chair stated that 'the Commissioners for Lunacy have to do something for their money' and the clerk was instructed simply to write to acknowledge the receipt of the letter. But the matter would not go away and after a further inspection in November the Commissioner noted that 'none of his recommendations had been listened to'. There was still only one chair in the day room and the rest comprised of hard benches. He recommended the following improvements:

- Provision of several low chairs with reclining backs for the day room and the retreat wards for the use of epileptics to prevent them hurting themselves during a fit.
- Games of entertainment or entertaining magazines for their perusal.
- The Guardians to make arrangements for this class of person to be able to walk out in the country under the care of the respective superintendent.

As we have already seen, the Sheffield Guardians did not always conform to the wishes or suggestions of the Poor Law authorities or the Commissioner for Lunacy. In October 1866 the Guardians took the step of enlarging the Kelham Street lunatic wards to bring back the lunatics from Wakefield Asylum. The reason was a financial one, as to maintain a lunatic at Wakefield cost the ratepayers 9s each whereas to have them at the workhouse would cost 3s 6d a week, almost two thirds less. It was estimated that there were thirty or forty such cases at Wakefield at that time, and they were all transferred to Sheffield that same month. However, with such a step the Guardians had made several additions for the comfort of the inmates. The following week another Commissioner, Mr Nairn, reported that: 'in the retreat wards at that time there were 78 people classed as lunatics, imbeciles or idiots and many were epileptic. There were 33 men and 45 women all quiet and orderly and there were no complaints'. He stated that 'he had requested more help for the two asylum assistants Mr and Mrs Hicks but his request had been ignored'. However, he was pleased to report 'that several comfortable chairs had been supplied in the day room and there were prints on the walls and periodicals for the inmates to read'. He reported that he had checked the hospital beds, which were found to be clean and tidy.

At the next Board meeting the chair said that he had spoken to the matron, Miss Day, to ask whether Mr and Mrs Hicks needed any help in the lunatic wards, but she told him that help could be supplied if it was needed. The Guardians congratulated themselves on the enlargements for the comfort of the lunatics. The chair noted to the Board that a few years ago Mr Farnall had wanted to erect a large lunatic asylum for the towns and districts of Rotherham, Doncaster, Ecclesall, Ecclesfield and Wortley. Instead, the Board had taken no notice and was rewarded with the fact that the lunatics of Sheffield were very well looked after indeed within the workhouse itself.

The asylum wards at Fir Vale, when they were opened in 1878, were described as being on the south side of the chief block separated by a 40ft wide road. The central part included a dining room with separate buildings for imbecile men and women. At last the Guardians had taken on board the criticisms of the dark and gloomy wards at Kelham Street, as it was reported that:

> The building had been arranged with every desire to ameliorate the condition of the unfortunate beings that need shelter within its walls. The east part was for 100 imbecile males and the west part was for eighty female imbeciles. Behind those buildings were courtyards where the more harmless inmates could take exercise.

Finally it seems that there had been an attempt to provide work for the inmate – washhouses for the women and workshops for the men – to provide constant employment. Nevertheless, the reporter stated that 'the extensive grounds, day rooms and workshops all needed constant supervision for this class of inmate'. In June of 1890 the Guardians were told that there were not enough people from the body of the workhouse to use as asylum attendants. After a conversation with the master, it was initially agreed that, as he already had three paid asylum attendants, the current arrangements should be sufficient. They later changed their minds, and it was decided that two more assistant nurses should be employed. Adverts were inserted in the *London Daily Telegraph and Local Government Chronicle* for Saturday 28 June requesting that all applications be received by 8 July. It was perhaps very fortunate that extra staff had been supplied, as it was not long before the death of another lunatic was reported.

On 23 August 1890 William Copley, the asylum nurse, told the master that a male patient had died during the night, at 3.15 a.m. The matter was reported to the Guardians,

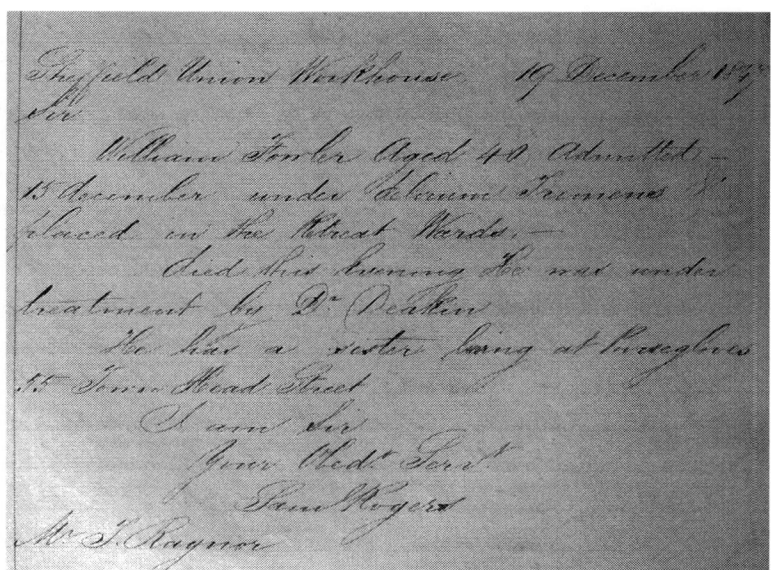

Notice of death of William Fowler.

as it seems that Copley had found night nurse, Robert Mayne, asleep in a spare room. As a consequence, the patients had been left unattended. Robert Mayne was summoned before the Guardians. They listened to his testimony, and then gave him the option of resigning. Failing that, he would be discharged. It was inevitable that further abuses would occur due to the lack of supervision: the staff were mainly untrained people, supplemented by workhouse inmates, taking care of the most vulnerable class of paupers. In May 1893 the master brought before the Guardians the case of Isaac Knapp, a pauper from the male asylum ward. He told them that he had suspended one of the asylum attendants, Frank Grosvenor, for ill-treating and assaulting this patient. He told them that the attack had been witnessed by another inmate, Samuel Green. It seems that Grosvenor had attacked Knapp while he was occupied in making a bed. Grosvenor went up to the victim and, with no provocation, boxed his ears; he then grabbed him by the throat and shook him, and finally kicked him as he fell to the ground. There were no reasons given for this violent attack. He also told the Guardians that this was the second complaint about the man's aggressive behaviour. He had been described as having a 'short temper and [as being] unfit for the position'. The Guardians praised the master for his prompt response, and they recommended that Grosvenor be dismissed from his office without delay.

There were many complaints about the retreat ward staff, which was inevitable given the job they had to do. But occasionally the Minutes reveal Cupid was present even in this unlikely setting. In August 1890, the same William Copley approached the Guardians to ask permission to marry Nurse Clara Matilda Elam. The Guardians reminded him that married couples were not to be employed together, and he told them that he was intending to apply for the joint post of master and matron at Penistone workhouse. He therefore asked the Guardians for a testimonial. The clerk was instructed to give a good testimonial to both of them. However, it seems that he was unsuccessful in his application, as he continued to work at the Fir Vale workhouse. In March 1892 another asylum attendant appeared before the Guardians to answer questions about his recent nuptials with another asylum nurse, named Sykes. The Guardians reminded him that they couldn't employ both him and his wife, and asked what he proposed to do about it. He told them that they also were applying for joint appointments as master and matron, but that if they were unsuccessful his wife would resign. The Guardians were happy with his resolution.

The asylum staff were criticised once again in the master's report of 5 November 1890. The master reported that about 10 p.m. the previous night a man named Martin Brannon, aged forty-nine and an inmate of the imbecile wards, was seized with a sudden outburst of excitement and became very violent, threatening to murder anyone who prevented him from leaving the building. From the evidence the master had received, a night attendant, George Henry Mitchell, became so terrified that he allowed Brannon to go out of the ward. He was followed to the gate and finally brought back to the wards, and the following morning the master had sent him to Wadsley. The Guardians appointed the visiting committee to investigate the matter and report back. George Mitchell attended the investigation and he agreed that he had been so scared by Brannon that he had opened the door and allowed him to escape. Two other asylum attendants, the just-married William Copley and James Mycock, were also questioned and it was resolved that Mitchell was very much to blame in allowing Brannon to leave the building. The Guardians discussed the findings and they recommended that Mitchell be cautioned as to his future conduct and he was reprimanded by the chair of the Guardians.

Unfortunately, however, that was not the end of the matter. The master put in a further complaint about Mitchell in February 1892. He claimed that whilst he was inspecting the wards he found that the man had locked the door to the imbecile ward and left the key in the lock. Mitchell was once more brought before the Guardians and he spoke about his previous experience with Brannon escaping and said he had locked the door as a precaution. He assured the Guardians that it was the first time he had left the key in the door, but they had no option but to order him to resign.

It seems that sometimes the patients in the retreat wards had been neglected not by a member of staff but by the Medical Officers themselves. It had been the practice that when Dr Hunt, the workhouse Medical Officer, was unable to attend the patients in the asylum then another Medical Officer, Mr Somerville, would attend in his place. It seems that this system broke down in April 1891 when the two Medical Officers were ordered to attend the Guardians' meeting to give their account of this negligence. Dr Somerville told the Guardians that in Mr Hunt's absence he had visited the asylum wards on the previous Sunday morning following a case of attempted suicide. He had asked one of the nurses if any of his patients had required his attention and was told not. He told the Guardians that it was his practice to attend the asylum patients only when he knew that one of them needed his attention or when he was sent for. The Guardians told him in no uncertain terms that he had to visit the asylum every day when he knew that Dr Hunt would be unavailable.

After the enlargements to the wards, and the bringing back of the lunatics to Fir Vale workhouse, the numbers began to rise. The problems of overcrowding in October of 1889 resulted in the more dangerous lunatics being sent back to the two asylums. Regular committee visits were undertaken by the Guardians to both asylums to examine the condition of the imbeciles and lunatics who were being paid for by the Sheffield Guardians. Incredibly, one such visit that month found 294 patients from Sheffield, 149 female and 141 male; the other four were children. They were all inspected, and the committee were impressed that the 'condition of the patients were most satisfactory and their general surroundings leave nothing to be desired'. Nevertheless, the attention of the Guardians was drawn to the alarming increase in the numbers of patients now chargeable to Sheffield. The committee told the Guardians that there were seventy-one more patients than seen on the previous visit, undertaken on 9 April 1890. The large numbers of Sheffield patients had made the asylum at Wadsley very overcrowded.

In May of 1894, Dr Kay, the medical superintendent of Wadsley, asked the Guardians if they could take back some of the more docile imbeciles. He was told that 'this Board is not prepared to receive any patients back', pointing out that 'most were sent under order from Dr Walker, the Visiting Commissioner of Lunacy and they were unable to countermand his orders'. But the overcrowding at Wadsley continued and the Sheffield Guardians were determined not to compromise their position. Only a few months later it was reported by the master that three lunatics who had been sent to Wadsley had been returned to Fir Vale workhouse. The three lunatics had been ordered to go by the Commissioner for Lunacy, and the master pointed out that there were in fact two more lunatics waiting to be dispatched to the asylum. The Guardians felt that it was the responsibility of Dr Kay to make alternative arrangements for the Sheffield lunatics and they instructed the clerk to send a copy of their resolution to Dr Kay, which stated that:

> steps should be immediately taken for the removal of these five patients to Wadsley and if certified by the Justices and refused admission by the superintendent of Wadsley, he be requested to communicate with such other County Asylums as he may think likely to find room for them with the view to their being sent to such as may seem desirable.

A report was received by the Guardians from the Commissioner for Lunacy, Dr Needham, in August of 1896, questioning the need for some of the Sheffield patients to be in Wadsley at that time. He stated that there were: 'some of the aged persons whose only mental infirmity appears to consist of weakness of the mind resulting from decay and some of the epileptics in whom there is no obvious mental disease associated with their fits and need scarcely to have been classed as insane at all.'

The Guardians responded that 'these patients are better cared for in the asylum than in the body of the workhouse owing to their requiring much more attention than could be given by ordinary inmates'. The overcrowding continued and the Guardians received two more letters from the Clerk of the Peace and the County Council in October 1898, laying out the terms to which the Guardians might agree to have the more harmless imbeciles back at Fir Vale from Wadsley. By this time – and due possibly to the overcrowding in the County Lunatic Asylums – the County Council made payments for the maintenance of lunatics and imbeciles held in workhouses and asylums. Despite this, the Guardians would not sanction any of their imbeciles to be returned back to Fir Vale:

This committee is agreed that the proposed arrangements appear to be surrounded by so many difficulties in the way of keeping books and records and taking into consideration the small number of patients which could be received into the workhouse asylum the Board are recommended not to proceed any further in the matter at this present time. The committee is hoping to hear that the asylum authorities have provided an extension of accommodation for patients and they trust that the asylum authorities will not press the Guardians of this union to receive any cases into the workhouse as they already have a much larger proportion of lunatics that any other workhouses in the West Riding.

A further discussion was held in July 1898 – followed by yet another request for some of the more docile imbeciles to be returned to Fir Vale. Mr Wycliffe Wilson stated that these asylums were refusing to take any workhouse inmates, yet the overcrowding had been caused by them taking in private patients in establishments built to accommodate the poor. He said that he understood at that point that Wadsley had a large number of private inmates from Lincolnshire and other counties, yet it had been established for patients from Yorkshire. In fact, the overcrowding had resulted in the asylum authorities writing to the relatives of the private patients asking for them to be returned; they had refused, and so now they were trying to get rid of the paupers. The chair stated that the only way in which they would accept the Sheffield imbeciles back was if the authorities would pay for them at the same rate at which they now paid to the authorities at Wadsley.

In October 1898 the deputation which regularly visited the asylums to check that their own patients were being well cared for visited Wadsley. They reported back to the Guardians that one of the patients had enquired about church services. Her name was Mary Jane McGlann, and she complained that she was an epileptic and was unable to go to church services whilst she had been at the asylum. She was Roman Catholic, and it was part of her duty to attend church at certain times of the year. The committee reported that there were at that time 100 Roman Catholic patients, all of whom were capable of attending a service if one could be provided. The Guardians resolved to do what they could and a copy of a resolution supporting the provision of church services at Wadsley was forwarded to the Home Secretary to that effect. One of the Guardians pointed out that the Home Secretary should make some provision as even convicts in prisons were allowed to attend services of their own denomination. There is no record of his reply but this does illustrate the lives of epileptics imprisoned in lunatic asylums, a condition which is easily treatable today.

Thankfully, more is understood about mental illness today and many illnesses are now treatable with medicine that was unavailable during the Victorian era. The treatment of the Sheffield pauper lunatics and imbeciles was no better or worse than any other town or city of the time. Shockingly, many of the inmates of the retreat wards were single women who had had children and were therefore treated as morally unsound. They were shunned by society, and the only refuge was within these wards.

thirteen

The Workhouse Inmates

In my research into workhouses a voice that is rarely heard is that of the inmates themselves. Two workhouse letter books, dating from 1847–1861, still exist in which the master or clerk copied letters and notes from the workhouse officials to various people which mention, sometimes very briefly, the inmates. This book is well worth studying by anyone interested in the Sheffield workhouse. It shows the hard lives of the paupers and their terrible existences inside and outside of the workhouse. But most importantly of all, it shows that the majority of people who entered the workhouses were not the idle shiftless sort reported by the Guardians and the Poor Law authorities but ordinary people like you or me. Of course, there were people, as we have already seen, who were too lazy to work, but many others were there through no fault of their own. Most of the notes and letters show a life in the workhouse which was not only hard and basic but also blighted by the antagonism felt by one officer towards another.

The speed with which the master had to report the death of any inmate to Mr Raynor is shown in a note written in February 1848. Mr Rogers told him that Charles Dyson, aged sixty-eight, had 'just died'. He describes the very sudden death, as the man was 'bleeding from the nose and mouth' ten minutes before. The master had sent for the Medical Officer but was told 'just now' that the man was dead. He reported that he had been quite well and cheerful all day, and employed in cutting bread for the inmates; he had been described as hearty and well, 'more than usual if possible'. The man had always had a cheerful disposition. The man's wife, who was blind, was also in the workhouse, and he told Mr Raynor that he had 'been with her today in good spirits'. One of his friends, a Mr Barker of Gleadless, had visited Dyson that day and the master wrote a letter to inform him of his friend's death. He wrote:

> You had not left here more than half an hour after spending a few hours with us… when I was astounded by the report that Charles Dyson with whom you were conversing this evening was dead from the rupture of a blood vessel and he was bleeding profusely from the nose and mouth. What a sudden transition – one hour so cheerful and happy – now dead. We must have an inquest on Monday and you must endeavour to be in town and

present at the inquest. Send me word by the bearer where I shall send for you when I know what time the inquest will be held.

Another sad note was sent to Mr Raynor in February 1849 stating that Thomas Penthorpe, aged forty-four, a shoemaker by trade who had been admitted the previous week, 'has just terminated his life by jumping out of the window of the hospital here. The man had only been at the workhouse a few days and during that time he had been treated by the resident Medical Officer Mr Benjamin Micklethwaite'. A further death of a lunatic in the retreat ward was reported on 5 January 1848. Mr Rogers wrote that Matthew Fearn, aged sixty-three, had died at 1.15 p.m that day. Fearn had gone into the workhouse at Kelham Street on 11 November after being sent there by the magistrates who had found him in 'a dangerous and destitute state'. He reported that his wife was a hawker by trade and travelled around the country; he told Mr Raynor that the last time he had seen her she had come from Manchester to visit him, and that Mr Raynor had no idea where she could be found to inform her of her husband's death.

It would seem that it was sometimes the responsibility of the Medical Officer to report a death. A letter was sent by Mr Skinner in October 1858 to the Town Hall where he described the death of Mercy Dunwell, a servant of the master, Mr Rogers. At 11.15 p.m. he was sent for, but by the time he got there she was dead. She had collapsed at 11 a.m., moaning and in great pain. The master had ordered her to be taken to bed and sent for Mr Skinner. She had been given a little brandy, but died very soon afterwards. Mercy Dunwell had been in the house for only four months and it was reported that she was a tramp. Mr Skinner recorded the death to the coroner at 'midnight in the master's office' and stated that at that time he had no suggestion as to what was the cause of death. He had never had cause to examine her during the time she was at the workhouse. Then Mr Rogers wrote a letter to a rector in Kent, the contents of which tell us more about Mercy. After her death, a prayer book had been found containing her name and an address of a rectory at Chelsfield in Kent. Mr Rogers wrote to inform the rector of Mercy's death at the age of about fifty-nine years, and asked, if she had any friends in the area, that he let them know of her death. He told the rector that:

She has for some time been employed as my domestic attendant in which capacity she has always merited my satisfaction and esteem. She was in the act of removing the tray from my supper table last night in her usual good health and spirits. She was immediately taken powerless, laid down the tray and fell moaning with a sensation of inward pain. Her circumstances changed to a death-like appearance. Restoratives were applied but without effect and before medical aid could be found she was a corpse.

He told the rector that an inquest was to be held the following Tuesday. Mr Skinner had by now completed a post-mortem and found that she died from 'concentric hypertrophy of the heart'.

One of the workhouse inmates, who died in the workhouse in April 1839, had apparently been quite a character in his youth. The *Sheffield Directory* records the death of John Blackwell, fifty-three, who had been in the workhouse on Kelham Street for eight years. He was a tailor and had been known as Jacky Blacker, or otherwise as 'King of the Gallery' of Sheffield Theatre, where he was very well known. On Tuesday, 3 December 1816 Jacky, aged twenty, he had distinguished himself in a bread riot which took place in Sheffield. These riots followed the battle of Waterloo when a trade depression hit England as a whole. Several towns demonstrated in what was known as 'the bread and blood riots' which swept the country. He had a loaf of bread impaled on a pole and smeared with blood to protest about the high costs of bread in the town. He was observed by James Stuart Wortley, the 1st Baron Wharncliffe, who dashed into the crowd of protesters and apprehended him. He was committed to take his trial at York Assizes on 19 March 1817, where he was found guilty and sentenced to two years in the Wakefield House of Correction. He was also charged at York Summer Assizes of 1820 for behaving in a riotous manner in Sheffield and encouraging other disorderly persons to riot, having in his possession a loaded pistol, a pike and other unlawful weapons. For this second offence he was sentenced to two and a half years' hard labour. What a shame that this wonderful character had spent his last eight years at Kelham Street.

The saddest notes in the letter book are the reports of the death of children. In November 1847, Mr Rogers informed Mr Raynor that a child of only a few months old was found dead in bed by its mother in the receiving ward of the workhouse. He noted that as the child had not received medical attention that Mr Raynor would need to contact the coroner to arrange an inquest. Unfortunately there is no evidence about the inquest or the reason why the child died, although not many children survived into the second or third year during the Victorian period. One death of a child at the Kelham Street workhouse was due to the inexperience of a nurse. On 2 April 1859 the Medical Officer, Mr Skinner, gave evidence at the inquest regarding the case of a month-old baby who had died at the workhouse. Mr Skinner said that he had been called to the hospital the previous evening to see a child named William Wilson and found him in a state of collapse after being given some medicine by a nurse 'without my knowledge or consent'. Nurse Mary Ann Graham, who was in the lying-in ward, had given him the medicine earlier that afternoon. The baby became ill and the Medical Officer was sent for about 8 p.m., but the child did not recover. It died about 7.15 a.m. the following morning. The death was due to an overdose of anodyne, which was a common painkiller used during that period. The jury recorded a case of accidental death and Nurse Graham was dismissed for her incompetency and carelessness. There is little doubt that Nurse Graham was acting in the best of reasons, but to act without the sanction of the Medical Officer was complete folly.

It was also part of the master's duty to notify relatives when inmates were not expected to live. A curious letter was written from Mr Rogers to Ann Irlam, 2 Ledger Street, Miller Court, Manchester in November 1847 regarding another William Wilson and stating that:

Mr William Wilson is not aware that I know his case and is not aware that you have written to enquire about him and is also not aware that I have replied. He wished (I understand) I should remain in ignorance of his real name and whilst he has been so ill I have chosen to know nothing respecting him but his care and comfort so far as I could promote it. He is not worse this morning but too ill to hold out hopes of his ultimate recovery to usefulness. I enclose you the means of reaching here if you would like to come.

It seems that Mr Wilson had a secret that he wished to keep! Another note, written to Mr Raynor on 24 November 1847, mentioned the death of Benjamin Shane, aged fifty, who had died of fever 'this night'. He had been admitted to Kelham Street workhouse under circumstances of great exhaustion a few days earlier, stating that he had travelled from Rotherham where his late master and his wife had died of the fever. He had caught the fever and had applied for relief at Rotherham but had been refused as his settlement was at Sheffield and it had taken him six hours to travel the distance of eight miles. A further victim of fever, Thomas Finnemore, died on 21 January 1848 and a letter was sent to his relative the same morning. The master informed Joseph Finnemore that his brother Thomas had asked him to inform him if he did not recover. The master had given instructions that Thomas be interred at the Sheffield Cemetery the following day, 22 January, at 4 p.m.

Despite the diligence of Mr Rogers, mistakes did happen, as when a workhouse inmate died before his wife could be notified. The master received a note from Mrs Hutton inquiring why her husband had been buried without her being notified of the matter; this occurred on 17 January 1860. The master wrote back, informing her that Thomas Hutton had been admitted to the workhouse on 15 December and had died on 8 January. He told her that he had asked him repeatedly whether he had any relatives or not so that he could let them know how he was, but Hutton had told him that he could do that for himself. Rogers told her that one of the paupers, acting as an under nurse, had been given some money by Hutton to buy ½lb butter, 1lb sugar, 2ozs of tea and six oranges and some apples for him. The same pauper left on 7 January, probably when he could see that Mr Hutton would not recover, and took what was left with him. Mr Hutton was buried in Sheffield General Cemetery on 11 January without his wife's knowledge. This does raise the question of exactly how much effort was put into finding the relatives of people who died in the workhouse, but without further evidence we can never be sure.

The letter book reveals that several of the paupers arrived at the workhouse with notes addressed to the master asking for them to be admitted to the house, which thankfully were faithfully copied into the letter book. These notes indicate that there were many respectable people of the town who were admitted to the workhouse. Mr W. Bruce of Rock Street wrote such a note on 6 November 1848; 'the bearer of the note' was Sarah Oxspring of 5 Osborne Street, who had seven children aged from twenty-three to three years of age. He said that the two oldest sons:

pay her 8s a week for board and lodgings. The next two are girls and have not been able to earn more than 2s 6d a week between them. The next boy is very seriously ill and has been so for seven weeks. The two youngest are aged six and three and are entirely dependent on their widowed mother who is not able to earn anything worth mentioning.

He asks Mr Rogers if he can ask the relieving officers for an allowance for her at least until the son gets better and is able to earn some more money for her. Another note was sent in May of 1849 from the minister of Queen Street Chapel to the master regarding 'the bearer' Martin Doyle, who was a native of Ireland. The minister describes him as a 'worthy and upright man who is educated and has in his possession very superior testimonials'.

Letter regarding Sarah Oxspring.

Although Doyle was willing to work in any capacity, the minister suggested to the master that he would prefer assisting as a teacher for the workhouse boy's school. He begs the master to assist him if he could to obtain such a post 'even if it was just for a week or two'.

The following statements from two sisters, copied into the letter book, are very sad, and tell us more about what life was like for some married women of the town. The first statement is dated 3 May 1849 and is from a woman named Sarah Cooper. She states that she and her baby were admitted to the Kelham Street workhouse on 28 August 1848 and discharged 'by her own desire' on 11 September 1848; the cause of her admittance was the neglect of her husband, Benjamin Cooper, and his ill-use of her. It seems, from the following tale, that the husband had mental-health issues. When she left the workhouse her husband was with her and she describes how he put his hand in his pocket for his knife and she said that 'if his knife had been there he would have stuck me and my child'. On her way into the town he threatened that they were going 'on the tramp' and told her that he would drag her to all the vagrant wards across the country whilst looking for work. He informed her, 'I should have no other accommodation'. Mrs Cooper states that 'she was in fear of him – indeed I always am'. She had run away from him for two or three months but had been forced to go back. Cooper had arrived once more at the workhouse on 21 December 1848, where she had been advised to go by her sister Charlotte Bingham of 14 Trinity Street, Sheffield. She had no food apart from a little bit that her sister had been

Statement of Sarah Cooper.

able to spare her. Mr Cooper, who had been an engine tenter by trade, had not worked for over a year and he went to the workhouse to stop her from entering with the two children. He threatened his wife that 'if she went into the house it would be the worse for her'. In order to prevent her from entering the workhouse her husband went upstairs to where the Guardian's Board meeting was taking place and her sister persuaded her to take this opportunity to go into the workhouse, which she did. She told the receiving officer that she was afraid of her husband and that 'he seems pretty well in his mind sometimes and at other times is violent and in such a state of mind as to put me in fear of my life'. Mrs Cooper told him that on one occasion he ran down the street after her with an open penknife in his hand threatening to stab her.

Her sister Charlotte also made a statement, which was recorded in the book. She states that six weeks previously she had gone to the workhouse with her sister, despite the fact that Mrs Cooper's husband attempted to stop them. Knowing that she 'had nothing to eat or any means of support', she advised her sister to gain admittance to the house. Mrs Bingham confessed that she was glad to see her sister in the workhouse where she would be 'free from want'. She then talked about her sister's life with her husband:

> I am of the opinion that Benjamin Cooper is too dangerous to be at large as he so often threatens to commit murder. On one occasion he got up in the night and went out leaving my sister crying. I went into the bedroom where I found an open razor and she told me that Cooper had threatened to kill her. He often made me fear that he would destroy my sister. Cooper has not worked regularly at anything for a year although he has now and then got a shilling by jobbing. Cooper has said many times to me that he would not work again and I believe that with such a state of mind as I have lately seen him he never will.

Thankfully an order was made out to have Benjamin Cooper detained and examined by the Medical Officer, who noted that due to the 'exceeding excited state of mind, from his very violent manner and from the fact that he has threatened to destroy his wife, I believe that his mind has become overtaxed and he is now insane and dangerous to himself and others'. It was reported that Mrs Cooper had been given no work to do in the workhouse as she was busy looking after both children who were 'poor and weak'.

There then, for some strange reason, follows a report which seems to have been written by a workhouse official on the meal enjoyed by the pauper inmates for Christmas. They describe the meal of roast beef and plum pudding and state how some of the Guardians had eaten with the inmates before the statement of Mrs Cooper continues. On 20 January 1849 she was given leave to go out of the workhouse. There she met with her husband, who was once more at large in Sheffield. When he had enquired about the health of the children she told him that Charlotte, the eldest child, had not eaten any plum pudding as she had been poorly. The statement, although interesting, gives no indication of why it was taken or why it was written in the letter book. However, further entries in the book show that a few days later Mrs Cooper and her two children were sent to the workhouse hospital, as both children had smallpox. On 26 January Mr Cooper arrived at the hospital and asked for an order to see his children. The master, knowing that he was dangerous, sent for the police, but no outcome is recorded. The next mention of the Coopers was an order issued on 2 August 1849 by the Medical Officer requesting that Benjamin Cooper 'be placed in a bed comfortably and to have warm bottles placed at his feet'. He also ordered 'extras' in the form of two pints of milk, and instructions that Cooper was to be given a meal of mutton chop and some more milk. It would seem by these extras that the man must have been in a state of near starvation or collapse. Obviously his mental health issues had not abated, as on the 7th he was dispatched to Wakefield Lunatic Asylum. Sadly, the next mention of him comes nine years later when a letter from Benjamin Cooper to the Poor Law Board is copied which requests that the Board open an enquiry into the death of his son, William Joseph Cooper, who died at the workhouse on 18 May 1857. He asked 'for the sake of justice and humanity' to let him have a hearing, and told them:

I have great reason to believe that that the child was greatly neglected. The master would not allow me to see the child two days before he died. My wife has also been removed out of the way to Belper Union without my knowledge. I wish My Lord and Gentlemen to have an inquest on the subject together with your advice on the same as to how I am to proceed.

He goes on to state that he had applied to the house committee to have the case brought before the Guardians, but that one of the Guardians, Mr Ashberry, 'would not allow it for reasons best known to himself'. He also alleged that the master had turned the child out of the hospital a few days before its death without the knowledge of the surgeon.

Mr Rogers, the master, was asked to explain his actions. He had previously told the Guardians that Benjamin Cooper, his wife Sarah and, by now, four of their children had been admitted to the workhouse, but the date had been left blank. He told them that on 1 April 1857, Cooper had been charged with a violent assault on an aged inmate and ordered to be taken before a magistrate, carried out on the following day; Cooper was then committed to prison. Before he was sent to Wakefield House of Correction the master had sent a message to the Town Hall, where the man was being held, asking him if he wanted to see his wife and child. The answer was that 'he had no desire to see them'. Mrs Cooper and the child, aged fourteen months, had been admitted straight to the hospital wards because the mother was suffering from opthalmia and general weakness and the child was not weaned. Mrs Cooper remained with the child until 15 April, when it died. On 6 April Mrs Cooper had been ill herself. The Medical Officer was sent for, and a further message had once again been given to Mr Cooper with permission to see his wife. Once again he had replied that 'he would not see her'. Despite Cooper's statement, Mr Rogers therefore insisted that he had never refused permission to see his wife. On 12 May, Mrs Cooper and her three children were sent to Belper workhouse by the Sheffield overseers. The following day Mr Cooper returned to Kelham Street from prison; he was also was removed to Belper the following day. The Medical Officer, Mr Skinner, appeared before the Guardians and he told them that he had attended Mrs Cooper and the child on their admittance to the hospital until the child's death, and later tended to Mrs Cooper until her removal to Belper. The cause of death had been spasmodic croup which he said was 'constitutional in the child'. He assured the Guardians that the child had received all the necessary attention up to the point of his death. There is no doubt that Benjamin Cooper had severe mental–health problems and that as a consequence of this led his wife and children a 'dog's life'. In the days before divorce became more available she would have had no option but to put up with it. Thankfully, the workhouses of the day did separate her from her husband, no doubt giving her and the children a little respite and regular, albeit uninspiring, meals.

As well as writing letters about the inmates the letter book shows that the master seems to have received quite a few letters enquiring about people in the workhouse. There is a reply by the master to Revd H.C. Sellers in Essex on 31 May 1848 regarding an inmate named Deanna Aves. Revd Sellers had previously written to Mr Rogers asking to be informed if this woman should apply for relief at Sheffield. The master replied that the woman had been in the diseased ward for several weeks. He told him that she had confessed to living as a prostitute in the town for some years. The Medical Officer had reported that it was a very distressing case of neglected syphilis, and despite the fact that she was anxious to leave the workhouse he promised Revd Sellers that he would detain her until he had received a reply from him. Another enquiry from Derby union was received by the master in October 1847. In reply he wrote:

Dear Sir. Mary Gaskill or Gaskin and a girl were admitted here on Thursday last and she died today. The child states that her father died in Derby. He was a hawker of needles and he came from Manchester. Can you give me any information respecting them? The child says her father died with you about two years ago.

Unfortunately no letter was recorded in answer. But another letter of enquiry was made by a firm of solicitors, Messrs J. Mason of York, on 24 September 1858 asking if the wife and children of Joseph Parrott were in the Kelham Street workhouse. The couple had run a public house in York, but Mr Parrott was now in prison for debt and his wife and children were penniless. The master replied that 'they were indeed at present in the workhouse and that the Guardians had urged him to notice their opinion of the hardship of this case in connection with the keen sensibility of Mrs Parrott at the humiliating position she and the children find themselves in here'. The poor woman must have been a sorry state for the Guardians to particularly mention it.

Another cry for help came from an inmate who wrote pityingly to her husband:

My dear husband,

I am here in this workhouse and am quite destitute so that I cannot leave unless you will be so good as to send me as much money as will pay my fare up to you. I think you had better send it in postage stamps. By enquiring at the post office there they will tell you how much it will be. Write by return of post. I am, dear husband, your affectionate wife, Maria Jowitt.

The letter was addressed to Samuel Jowitt in the care of Patrick Gallevan, porter, Ludborough Station near Louth.

There is no doubt that many paupers absconded from the workhouse. This in itself was not a crime, but if they absconded wearing the workhouse clothing then they could be sent before the magistrate. They would be charged with stealing the workhouse clothes, seen as belonging to the Guardians. Such a pauper was mentioned in a letter sent to Mr Rogers from the 'Woburn lockup' from Mr R. Young, the superintendent of police there, informing him that they had detained a man named John Alexander. When the man was questioned he was found to have in his possession a fustian jacket labelled Sheffield Union. He described the man as being aged about forty-five years of age, 5ft 9ins in height, of a dark complexion with black whiskers. He asked Mr Rogers to reply immediately if there were any charges to be made against him as there was no other case against him and he would have to be discharged. Mr Rogers wrote back the same day stating that the man was probably George Acaster, a joiner with defective sight who he described as being thin and having a dark complexion. He told the police superintendent that he had gone after the man who had been wearing workhouse clothes and caught up with him in Derbyshire, but having no warrant had been forced to let him go. No doubt the man would have been charged and brought back to Sheffield, where he would be sent to prison by the magistrates. A typical sentence for this particular offence would probably be three months in the Wakefield House of Correction.

Another letter was sent by the master in July 1860 to Mrs Sutting, the matron of the St James Asylum at Leeds. He told the matron that a poor woman, named Mrs Elizabeth Chubsey, in the Kelham Street workhouse had received a letter from her daughter, Ann, an inmate at Leeds. The daughter had expressed a wish to return to her mother, and asks the Sheffield workhouse authorities for the means to travel. He informed her 'that, Madam, is out of the question', the reason being 'that her mother was in too depressed a condition both in mind and body to be able to do anything for her daughter'. He told her that 'it would be remiss of me to intimate to her that any hopes she may entertain of support, assistance or even protection from her mother and she will probably be disappointed'. He then tells her, somewhat patronizingly, that the daughter is seriously recommended to 'step into the world again from the platform that she now occupies'. A reply was sent to him from the matron at Leeds stating that the daughter was:

…in a unhelpful state of mind, she is so very indolent and unthankful that I could not recommend her to any situation. I think that sometimes she is not altogether sane, as she talks so strangely about religion professing so much, but her conduct departs with this profession. What is to become of her I cannot say. She is certainly a case for the workhouse. Our community will not turn her out unless she is unwilling to stay and we have no power to retain her.

In January of 1860 the Guardians and the local police were strongly criticised by a local coroner for their attitude to the poor people when they had allowed a man to be transported to the workhouse in a wheelbarrow. The man was called Edward Hobson and he had died at Kelham Street the following day. Hobson was formerly employed as a collector for the Sheffield Gas Co. but since the death of his wife two years previously had 'led a completely intemperate lifestyle' and had reduced himself to a condition of extreme wretchedness. He was taken before the magistrates on Wednesday 4 January on a charge of being drunk and incapable – where, for some unstated reason, he was 'set at liberty'. The following day he was found in Castle Street in a helpless state and was ordered to be moved to the workhouse. He died there the following day, on Friday 6 January. PC Patrick Duffy was called before the inquest, and told the jury that Sergeant Whytell had told him to take the man to the workhouse. He had tried to get him to stand up but Hobson was incapable of standing. Duffy had suggested a cab, but the sergeant told him that the man was in such a filthy condition that no cab man would have him. With the assistance of another constable named Allen, the man was taken to the workhouse in a wheelbarrow. Mr Skinner, the Medical Officer, said that when he was brought to the workhouse it was obvious that he was very ill indeed as he was completely paralysed. He had visited him on the Friday, where he was still in a state of collapse and obviously close to death as he died later that afternoon. Assisted by Mr Benson, Mr Skinner undertook the post-mortem and found that there was hardly a healthy organ in the whole of the man's body. He gave his opinion that the man had died from chronic disease of the lungs and the liver owing to 'intemperance and the inclemency of the weather'. PC Duffy was strongly criticised for the method of transportation and the coroner asked him if it would have been more humane to have carried him on a stretcher. The verdict of the jury was 'death due to intemperate lifestyle' and the coroner stated once again his abhorrence of the way that the man had been treated, stating that, 'I hope never to find police officers forgetting their duty again by transporting anyone through the streets like a log or a dead dog'.

These then are some of the inmates in the Sheffield workhouse and their lives within and outside of the walls. The Guardians of Sheffield might have been a contentious group of men, but they were not afraid of the Poor Law authorities and were not afraid of taking risks. Under their control they twice organised farms for the poor of the town to give them the kind of work that a man could do with dignity. They developed the very successful Scattered Homes schemes to take away the stigma of the workhouse for pauper children. In February of 1890 they took another major step when they decided that they would no longer use the services of the inmates in the workhouse hospital. Instead, the workhouse would be run on hospital lines, with the election of professional nurses. The women who wished to become nurses would be trained for three years, starting off as probationary nurses and attending lectures and examinations. The Medical Officer of Health, Dr Downes, sent a report to the Guardian's after his visit on 29 April 1890, when he reported:

> At the present time the administration of the Infirmary is in the transition stage of very important changes. The Guardians have I understand determined to do away with pauper help and all its attendant evils in nursing and are remodeling the nursing staff. It is intended there should be ten charge nurses (two on night duty) and nine probationary nurses (five for the day and four for the night shift) and the Guardians have provided a suitable nurses' home.

This revolutionary change would reverberate in the Poor Law workhouses of the country as gradually all workhouses would become hospitals. Nevertheless, it was a very forward and clear thinking decision for the Sheffield Guardians and the Local Government Board of that time.

Sheffield has put the stigma of the workhouse behind it and is now a prosperous and industrious city inviting people to visit its shops, museums and art galleries. Nothing of the workhouse now remains save Kelham Island Museum, which is built on the site of the old cotton mill. But the curiosity surrounding the lives of the paupers of Sheffield workhouse still exists, and information can be found in the archives and libraries of Sheffield. I would urge anyone who is interested in finding out more about the workhouse to look at what is available there. I have also added an appendix of some of the areas of study on this fascinating subject.

appendix one

Index

appendix two

Potential Sources

FOR FAMILY HISTORIANS

All from the Sheffield Archives, 52 Shoreham Street, Sheffield. Tel: 01142 203 9395. Email: archives@sheffield.gov.uk. Please contact them beforehand if you want to order any of the following, and please be aware this is only part of the material available.

Letters of the Sheffield Workhouse. Ref. No. CA24 (54–55). Letters written by master Samuel Rogers to various people mentioning names of inmates: some are difficult to read, but most are very readable and interesting. It also contains yearly lists of lunatic maintained by the Guardians in West Yorkshire Lunatic Asylum from 1850 onwards.

In July 1860 there is a list of fifty-one names of paupers who have been in the workhouse for a continuous period of five years and gives the reason why they are unable to maintain themselves. Some of these reasons are simply labeled 'idiot', 'infirm' and 'blind and infirm'.

Sheffield Guardians' Minutes for 1894/5, Ref. No. CA692/5. See page 298, which contains a list of fifty-nine apprentices taken out of the workhouse since 1879 and a potted history of outcomes and comments about their character.

Register of Children admitted to Sheffield Union Children's Homes, Herries Road, Fir Vale (Ref. No. CA41/33 for 1894-1902, and CA41 41/34 for 1903- 1910). These include dates of admission and discharge/name of person admitting them/what happened to them/names of adopted families/names of where apprenticed to. Easy to access as all the children's names are in alphabetical order.

Register of Children admitted to Sheffield Union Children's Homes, Herries Road, Fir Vale, 1910-1921 (Ref. No. CA41/35-36).

Masters' punishment book: Fir Vale Workhouse 1903-1926 (Ref. No. CA510/1). This book contains the names of paupers who have been punished, usually for coming back to the workhouse late after having passes to attend church. They are sometimes given bread and water for three meals and sometimes sent to D block (punishment block).

Register of Children Admitted to Ecclesall Union Fulwood Cottage Homes, 1905-1945 (Ref. Nos. CA41/37-38 and Acc. 2006/13, 2a-c).

Herries Road and Scattered Homes Registers, 1926-1939 (Ref. Nos. Acc. 2006/13, 3a-c).

Scattered Home Admission and Discharge Slips, 1940s-1950s (Ref. Nos. Acc. 2006/13, 8a-h).

Brightside Workhouse Census SY/245/k1/7.

1910-30 Admissions and Creeds Register.

Bibliography

PRIMARY SOURCE MATERIAL, ALL COURTESY OF SHEFFIELD ARCHIVES
UNLESS OTHERWISE STATED

Printed Poster: Remarks for the Best Site for the Workhouse, 5 May 1804 (Ref No 6296/
    L7-1).
Printed Poster: Answer to Above by Samuel Roberts, 5 May 1804 (Ref. No. 6296/L7-2).
Printed Poster: Listing Resolutions at the General Meeting held on 13 April 1804 (Ref. No.
    MD1123).
Masters' punishment book: Fir Vale Workhouse 1903-1926 (Ref. No. CA510/1).
List of Overseers of Sheffield 1608-1787 (Ref. no. CA26/1).
Sheffield Union Minute Books (Ref. No. CA 692/1- 8).
Sheffield Workhouse Letter Book (Ref. CA24 [54-55]).

SECONDARY SOURCE MATERIAL

R.J. Pye Smith: reprinted from the *Sheffield Daily Telegraph,* 4 Sept 1896, Ref. No. AC67-3.

NEWSPAPERS

Sheffield Mercury
Sheffield and Rotherham Independent
Sheffield Daily Telegraph
Rotherham and Masbrough Advertiser
Sheffield Iris

BOOKS

John Daniel Leader, *Records of the Burgery of Sheffield* (London, Sheffield Independent Press, 1897)

Sheffield Local Directory, published and sold by Robert Leader

Sheffield Independent 1830, courtesy of Sheffield Local Studies Library

W.H.G. Armytage, *Heavens Below: Utopian Experiments in England 1560-1960* (London, Routledge & Kegan Paul, 1961)

Lyn Howsam, *Memories of Life in the Workhouse and the Old Hospital at Fir Vale* (Published by ALD, 2002)

Other titles published by The History Press

Sheffield Crimes: A Gruesome Selection of Victorian Cases

MARGARET DRINKALL

This volume collects together the most shocking criminal cases from Sheffield's Victorian newspapers. These grisly cases will transport the horrified reader back to a time where horse-drawn carriages clattered through the streets of the city, and the town's gin palaces and music halls teemed with thieves, drunkards and fallen women. Filled with infamous historical cases - including grave robbing, murder, poisoning, bigamy, and daring jewel and garrotte robberies - it will fascinate residents, visitors and historians alike.

978 0 7524 5820 5

Rotherham Workhouse

MARGARET DRINKALL

This volume explores all aspects of life in that dread institution, the workhouse. From the staff who lived and worked here to the lunatics who were kept - sometimes unsuccessfully - in the medical wing, the babies and mothers whose lives began - and sometimes ended - in the maternity ward, and the tramps, families and destitute persons who passed through the doors every day, it reveals a side of Rotherham that has long since been forgotten. With more than fifty illustrations, it will fascinate residents and visitors alike.

978 0 7524 5290 6

Murder & Crime in Sheffield

MARGARET DRINKALL

The grim and bloody events in this book, many of which have not been written about for more than a century, reveal the dark heart of Victorian Yorkshire. Some of these gruesome tales would not look out of place in a work of fiction – a body abandoned in the middle of the street, a man murdered by his wife and her lover and a daring case of highway robbery. Richly illustrated with archive and modern photographs, this gruesome collection will fascinate anyone with an interest in Sheffield's dark past.

978 0 7524 5568 6

Murder & Crime in Rotherham

MARGARET DRINKALL

With stories ranging from child murders to brutal stabbings, the misdemeanours in this book promise to shock and fascinate in equal measure. While some of these felonies are unjustifiable, much of Rotherham's crime was the result of the desperate poverty that many of the area's inhabitants experienced. Illustrated with both rare images and archive reports, this volume shows just how difficult, and how brutal, life in Victorian England could be.

978 0 7524 5524 5

Visit our website and discover thousands of other History Press books.

www.thehistorypress.co.uk

Printed in Great Britain
by Amazon